CUBE
BOOK

WILDLIFE

WHITE STAR PUBLISHER

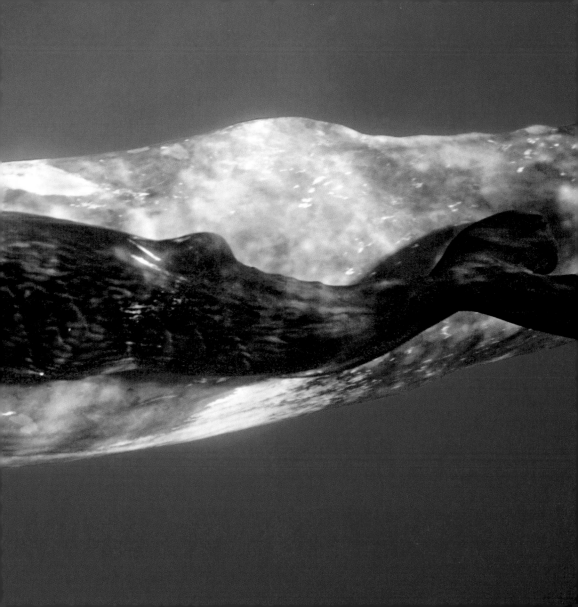

EDITED BY

VALERIA MANFERTO DE FABIANIS

texts by
CRISTINA MARIA BANFI
GIORGIO G. BARDELLI
ANGELA SERENA ILDOS
COLIN MONTEATH
CRISTINA PERABONI
FRANCESCO PETRETTI
ALBERTO LUCA RECCHI
RITA MABEL SCHIAVO

graphic design
CLARA ZANOTTI

editorial staff
GIADA FRANCIA
GIORGIA RAINERI

translation
text: MICHAEL FORMISANO
caption: CORINNE COLETTE

© 2007 **WHITE STAR S.P.A.**
VIA CANDIDO SASSONE, 22-24
13100 VERCELLI - ITALY
WWW.WHITESTAR.IT

● China. A panda cub with its mother.

ISBN 978-88-544-0195-2

REPRINTS:
1 2 3 4 5 6   11 10 09 08 07

Printed in China

CONTENTS

WILDLIFE

1 • French Guyana.
An Allobates frog.

2-3 • Kenya. A lioness
drinking.

4-5 • Russia. A Siberian
tiger.

6-7 • Antarctica. A colony
of emperor penguins.

8-9 • Alaska. Bears fishing
for salmon.

10-11 • Atlantic Ocean.
Sperm whales.

15 • Rwanda. A close-up
of a gorilla.

17 • Africa. Cheetahs
hunting.

19 • North America.
Polar bears.

20-21 • Falkland Islands.
An albatross colony.

22-23 • Florida. An
alligator in the Everglades.

24-25 • Namibia.
A gemsbok antelope.

FOREWORD   page   16

INTRODUCTION   page   26

LORDS OF THE SAVANNAH   page   40

THE GREEN INFERNOS   page   134

POLAR HABITATS   page   226

LIFE AMID THE DUNES   page   296

THE GREAT BLUE   page   352

LIFE ON THE PRAIRIES   page   488

IN THE SHADOW OF THE PEAKS   page   536

THE CALL OF THE FOREST   page   582

BETWEEN LAND AND WATER   page   652

BIOGRAPHIES, INDEX, CREDITS   page   728

Foreword

SUFFER. THIS IS A WORLD WHERE SURVIVAL OFTEN DE-
PENDS OF SOPHISTICATED STRATEGIES TO CONQUER A
TERRITORY, TO GAIN DOMINANCE OF A GROUP, TO DE-
FEND ONE'S LIFE OR ONE'S OFFSPRING. THE RULES ARE
CLEAR-CUT, SIMPLE AND THE SAME EVERYWHERE IN A
SORT OF UNIVERSAL LANGUAGE.

ROLES, TOO, ARE WELL DEFINED: THE STRONGEST ONE
WINS AND IT MAINTAINS ITS POWER ONLY AS LONG AS IT
CAN PROVE ITSELF TO BE THE STRONGEST. HERE,
THERE'S NO ROOM FOR SUBTERFUGE, POLITICAL GAMES
OR AMBIGUITY.

Valeria Manferto De Fabianis

Introduction

by Giorgio G. Bardelli

We will never be able to do enough to publicize the importance of protecting the environment and its living species; indeed, knowledge and management of the land, sea, and air and of life forms are of vital importance to the existence and well-being of humankind. Unfortunately though, all too often, environmental problems, both global and local, are closely related to human misery.

Human beings, among the unnumbered species that have evolved over the long course of the earth's history, seem to be the only ones not lim-

* Oceania. A white shark suddenly surfacing from the waters of the Pacific Ocean.

Introduction

ITED TO PERFORMING TASKS AIMED ONLY AT SURVIVAL: SECURING FOOD AND WATER, BREEDING, TAKING CARE OF OFFSPRING, DEFENDING THEMSELVES AND THEIR YOUNG FROM ATTACKERS, AND FIGHTING AGAINST ENVIRONMENTAL DIFFICULTIES. BIOLOGISTS EXPLAIN THAT THE AESTHETIC SENSE WHICH HAS DEVELOPED ALONG WITH THE CULTURAL EVOLUTION OF *HOMO SAPIENS*, WHO CREATED PALAEOLITHIC ART JUST AS IT ALSO CREATED CONTEMPORARY ART, LEADS US TO OBSERVE THE WORLD SURROUNDING US NOT ONLY FOR THE SAKE OF ENJOYMENT BUT, AS POETS WOULD SAY, TO UPLIFT THE MIND. UNDOUBTEDLY HUMAN LIFE IS CONNECTED TO THAT OF OUR PLANET THROUGH A COMPLEX ECOLOGICAL NET-

Introduction

WORK, BUT IT'S ALSO TRUE THAT HUMAN EXISTENCE STRIVES TO CONTEMPLATE BEAUTY AND SPLENDOR, ELEMENTS THAT THIS BOOK GENEROUSLY PRESENTS. AND IF THE EVOLUTION OF OUR SPECIES HAS TAKEN THIS PATH, GIVING US A SENSIBILITY FOR THE NATURAL WORLD, IT IS BECAUSE MOST OF OUR HISTORY HAS TAKEN PLACE IN NATURE, IN A CONSTANT MUTUAL RELATIONSHIP WITH THE WOODS, SAVANNAS, DESERTS, OCEANS AND MOUNTAINS. IN SOME INDIVIDUALS THIS KIND OF SENSIBILITY SEEMS TO BE MORE DEVELOPED THAN IN OTHERS, SO MUCH SO THAT THEY BECOME WILDLIFE AND NATURE PHOTOGRAPHERS. THE MOTIVES DRIVING THEM TO UNDERTAKE SUCH A FASCINATING YET HIGHLY CHALLENGING CAREER

Introduction

ARE VARIED; BUT THEY GENERALLY ARE AS FOLLOWS: TO ENGAGE PEOPLE'S INTEREST IN THE BEAUTY OF OUR PLANET AND THE VARIETY OF ITS ELEMENTS, THUS AIMING TO STIMULATE A HIGHER LEVEL OF AWARENESS AND OF THE NECESSITY TO TAKE THE UTMOST CARE IN ITS PRESERVATION.

WE ARE GRATEFUL TO THEM, BECAUSE THROUGH THEIR WORK WE ARE NOT MERELY INFORMED BUT ALSO IN-SPIRED IN A PROFOUND WAY TO PAY MORE ATTENTION TO OUR ORIGINS AND THE WORLD IN WHICH WE LIVE.

31 • Sumatra. An orangutan swinging in the trees of the tropical forest.

32-33 • Kenya. A leopard ready to devour a gazelle.

34-35 • South America. Sea-lions with bizarre expressions.

36-37 • North America. Aquatic plants are one of elk's favorite foods.

38-39 • North America. A wolf hunting in the cold Alaskan winter.

LORDS of the SAVANNAH

RITA MABEL SCHIAVO

Africa. Photographed at the end of a long yawn, this leopard is showing off its long fangs.

INTRODUCTION Lords of the Savannah

THE BLISTERING HORIZON. THE MEMORABLE AFRICAN SUNSETS ARE UNRIVALED, IT'S ALMOST AS IF THEY WANTED TO SNEAK INTO OUR THOUGHTS, CONFIDENT THEY WILL LEAVE AN UNFORGETTABLE MEMORY. AS THE SKY FADES AWAY, A FARAWAY ROAR SEEMS TO BEGIN A NEW NIGHT IN THE SAVANNA: WE, AS MERE VISITORS, ARE LEFT TO LISTEN TO DARKNESS WHILE COUNTLESS EYES SHINE REFLECTING THE DIM LIGHT OF THE STARS. THE REEDS BY THE RIVER RUSTLE AND BREAK UNDER THE WEIGHT OF A HEAVY HIPPOPOTAMUS WHO, NOW THAT THE SUN IS NOT SHINING, IS ABLE TO LEAVE ITS REIGN. A CHAOTIC PATTERING OF

INTRODUCTION Lords of the Savannah

HOOVES TELLS US THAT A PREDATOR HAS LAUNCHED HIS STRIKE.

MY SHORT SLEEP IS INTERRUPTED BY OUR GUIDE: WE MUST TAKE ADVANTAGE OF THE FIRST LIGHT. FLYING BIRDS CROSS THE BLUE SKY CLEFT BY THE MORNING CLOUDS, WHILE WITH THEIR CACKLE THE BABOONS ANNOUNCE THE NEW DAY. WE MANAGE TO GET CLOSE TO A GROUP OF LIONS: A THRILL RISES UP WITHIN US. EVEN THE YOUNGER ONES HAVE MUZZLES STAINED WITH BLOOD: LAST NIGHT THE HUNT WAS FRUITFUL FOR THE PACK. I TAKE A PICTURE OF THESE PROUD-MANED RULERS OF THE SAVANNA, NOW LOOKING ALMOST MILD AS TWO CUBS PLAY WITH THE

INTRODUCTION Lords of the Savannah

PLUMES OF THEIR TAIL. BUT THE STRUGGLE HAS BEEN EXHAUSTING AND ONLY THE GROUP ATTACK, AND THE LIONESSES' EXPERIENCE ENSURED THE CAPTURE OF A ZEBRA THAT MIGHT HAVE KICKED HER PREDATORS TO DEATH.

THE SURPRISES ARE NOT OVER; NEAR A POOL SOME ELEPHANTS ARE QUENCHING THEIR THIRST. WE GET CLOSE DOWNWIND. WE ARE NOT THE ONLY ONES TO WATCH THE GROUP WITH THE SEVERE- LOOKING MA-TRIARCH. AN IMPOSING MALE TRUMPETS NEXT TO A BAOBAB. I OBSERVE THE SILENT STRENGTH OF THESE TWO GIANTS: BOTH ANIMAL AND TREE SEEM IMPRE-GNABLE AND ETERNAL, READY TO FACE ANY ENEMY.

Lords of the Savannah
Introduction

THEY ARE THE UNDISPUTED RULERS OF THE SAVANNA.

ELEPHANTS ARE THE UNDISPUTED LORDS OF THE SAVANNAH AND THEY ARE VERY CLOSELY CONNECTED TO ITS LIFE CYCLE.

THE ELEPHANT FEEDS ON THE LEAVES OF THIS GREAT TREE AND ON ITS DELICIOUS FRUITS. IT CUTS THROUGH THE TRUNK OF THE TREE WITH ITS TUSKS LOOKING FOR SOFT MORSELS. ON THE OTHER HAND, IF THE BAOBAB SEEDS DIDN'T GO THROUGH THE DIGESTIVE SYSTEM OF THE ELEPHANT, THEY WOULD HAVE NO CHANCE OF SPROUTING.

● Africa. The trunk of the largest land animal can be used as an olfactory "periscope" and to sound trumpeting bellows to signal anger, defense or fear.

52-53 ● Africa. This young kudo, away from the herd, has been taken by surprise and is now desperately trying to escape a lioness.

53 ● A lioness has knocked down this young antelope and will kill it by biting its throat.

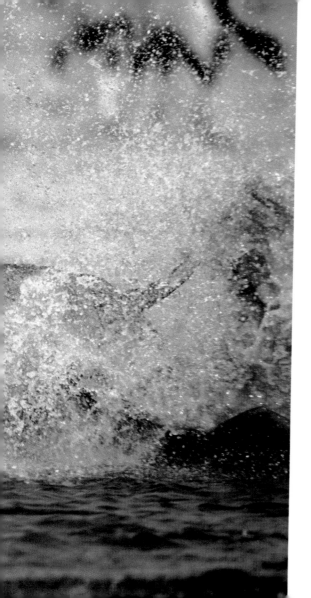

54-55 • Africa. River banks are often used for ambushes by predators: the patience of this lioness has been awarded and she will strike soon.

55 • Africa. Attacks are only successful if the lion's claws rake the antelope within 100 meters of the chase.

56-57 • Africa. Only the agility, courage and strength of a starving lioness can challenge one of the giants of the savannah: the buffalo.

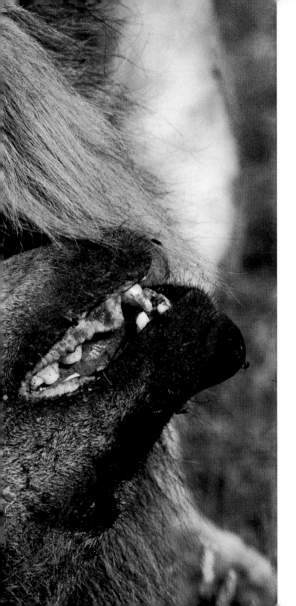

58-59 • Africa. Once it has its claws in its prey, the lioness will bite the throat of its prey to suffocate it.

59 • Africa. A lioness grasp its prey by the scruff of the neck.

60 • Africa. A lion cub learning to attack by practicing on the tails of the adult lions.

60-61 • Africa. Male lions can be good fathers and they often spend time playing with the cubs in the pride.

62-63 • Africa. This group of lions is relaxing in the grass to dry off after having taken a refreshing bath.

64-65 • Africa. Cheetahs are territorial animals and are only partially social. Males get together to hunt and to defend their territory.

66 and 67 • Africa. Cheetah cubs are always with their mother except when she is hunting. She brings a prey for them to taste when they are 5-6 weeks old.

68-69 • Africa. An unusual scene: a famished cheetah is hunting a zebra herd.

Africa. When the cheetah cubs are six months old, their mother brings them a captured animal which is still alive to teach them to kill and it mights take the cubs months to learn.

72 • The amount of energy needed to capture a prey is very great and, in addition, the cheetah must defend her 'catch' from numerous other animals.

73 • Africa.This time, a cheetah has been successful in chasing away a vulture but it must eat its meal in a hurry before the mighty and more numerous lions, hyenas and jackals arrive.

74 and 75 • Licking each other is a way to relax for felines.

76-77 • Africa. The cheetah is the fastest animal on land and moves at up to 115 km/h.

78-79 • Africa. Considered to be the architect of the savannah, the elephant spends about 16 hours a day eating, and limiting the overgrowth. It also transports seeds and removes trees.

80 ● Africa. This buffalo expresses its might as it suddenly appears through the high grasses of the savannah.

80-81 ● Africa. The African elephant frequently changes its habitat in search of food, water and shade.

Africa. The African elephant never stops growing and, therefore, the oldest elephants are the biggest ones. These giants can eat up to 300 kilograms of food every day.

Africa. This herd of elephants provides transport to cattle egret herons. These birds travel comfortably and easily find food in the soil moved by the elephants.

Africa. Elephants find it hard to escape the heat and insects of the savannah and a sand shower is the best solution.

88 ● Africa. Even though 'only children', baby elephants like to play with the other cubs in the herd.

88-89 ● Africa. The childhood of the earth's largest land animal lasts 6 years and males only leave the herd after they have turned 12 years old.

90 ● Africa. Height, speed and powerful, cutting-edged hooves keep adult giraffes safe from predators: the drinking place is the only truly dangerous spot.

91 ● Africa. There aren't many hierarchical battles between adult male giraffes though they express rivalry by trying to make their adversary lose its balance by weaving their long necks together pressing and twisting them.

92-93 ● Africa. A herd of giraffes stare at us from amongst thorn bushes. They stand out against the gray sky and are ready to run away if threatened.

94 and 95 ● Africa. Giraffes can eat more than 30 kilograms of vegetables per day.

96-97 ● Africa. Two zebras follow a gnu herd. These animals are talented at forecasting storms.

98-99 ● Africa. The crossing of rivers is a dangerous time for migrating gnus.

Africa. Moved by instinct, these gnu are forced to cross rivers full of dangerous Nile crocodiles which are up to six meters long. These are the largest crocodile species and they pose a great threat to the other animals in their environment.

Africa. This unlucky gnu has no chance of escaping the powerful bite of the crocodile which suddenly surfaced through the murky waters.

Africa. In the torrid savannah, the energy needed for fights between males is best found in the coolness of water. Only a dominant stallion can lead a zebra herd.

Africa. These impalas are relaxing as they drink while numerous cow buffaloes are ridding them of insects.

108 ● Africa. The gerenuk takes a standing position when eating leaves, shoots and fruits, usually of acacia trees. This gazelle species has never been observed eating grass.

109 ● Africa. These small herds of gerenuk comprise one male with various females and cubs. When they take a standing position, they can reach leaves up to 2 meters from the ground.

110-111 ● Africa. Gazelles give birth to their young in the grasses immediately after the rainy season.

111 ● Africa. Female impalas are always on alert. If attacked, the suddenly flee in all directions and this disorients their enemies.

112-113 • Africa. A white rhinoceros cub will stay with its mother for two or three years.

113 • Africa. Rhinoceroses are very shortsighted. Males challenge each other by crossing and touching each other's horns, but only when directly in front of them.

114-115 • Africa. Speed and a talent for camouflage weren't enough to ensure that this coluber escaped the agile serval.

115 • Africa. Solitary and territorial, this serval marks its territory like most felines do.

116-117 • Africa. Hyenas use sophisticated hunting strategies when the pack hunts together.

117 • A jackal and some vultures fighting over an abandoned carcass.

118 ● Africa. The social order of baboons is based on a rigid hierarchy. Males express dominance by opening their mouth, showing their fangs, lifting their eyebrows and widening their eyes.

119 ● Africa. The baboon can feed on trees or on the ground. It's an omnivore and sometimes it even enjoys an antelope cub.

120 ● Africa. Young male baboons stay with their pack for four years. They rank under their mother and have their own hierarchy.

121 ● Africa. The female baboon has a single baby and she dedicates half of her time to it for its first few months. Sometimes, alpha females steal the cubs of inferior ranking females.

122 • Africa. This jackal doesn't worry the giraffe; it continues its leisurely drinking.

122-123 • Africa. Doves are a difficult prey for these jackals, which are also fond of eating carrion.

124 • Africa. Hiding in the grass of the savannah, this leopard is moving close to its prey silently and down wind.

125 • Africa. When night falls, the eyes of felines shine in the dark because of their night vision, which allows even the weakest light to be magnified by the structure of their eyes.

• Africa. This panther is ready to leap on its prey and is getting as close as it can while carefully observing it ready to pick up its slightest signal.

● Africa. Mamma leopard spends at least half her time with her cubs for the first two months but after that period, she spends more and more time hunting to feed her family.

130 • Africa. Powerful muscles command the leopard's sharp and retractable claws. These claws enable the leopard to climb trees.

131 • Africa. Camouflaged among the branches of an acacia tree, this leopard can finally rest.

132-133 • Africa. The collapse of the market for leopard fur because of laws forbidding leopard hunting has allowed the number of these beautiful animals to increase.

The Green Infernos

Introduction

Rain forest, cloud forest, mist forest, flooded forest, jungle: in every language these terms evoke a shady world, made inaccessible by lianas and fallen tree trunks and branches, enveloped in a stifling atmosphere. It's not easy for people to move around in such an obstructed place, with visibility down to a few feet. The best moment to do so is at dawn, when hearing is the sense that guides us. Then, the roaring of the howler monkeys in South America, the hoarse sneer of the rhinoceros hornbill in Africa, the melodious singing of the gibbons in Asia greet the

- Asia. Fewer than 5000 tigers remain in India, Indochina, Indonesia and continental Asia, a small fraction of the almost 100,000 tigers present in Asia forty years ago.

INTRODUCTION The Green Infernos

SOUTHERN BASE BORDERS ABRUPTLY WITH THE BORANA AND OMO PLAINS. HERE THE SOIL IS RICH: ONE FIELD THERE CAN PRODUCE 1570 LBS (712 KG) OF GRAIN PER 2.5 ACRES (1 HECTARE), AND A COW GIVES 0.80 GALLONS (3 LITRES) OF MILK EVERY OTHER DAY, TREES ARE RARE AND MEN HAVE ALMOST FORGOTTEN WHAT A FOREST IS. FEW PEOPLE KNOW ABOUT THE EXISTENCE OF THIS CLOUD FOREST OF HAGENIA AND PODOCARPUS TREES, HEATHERS AND GIANT JUNIPERS, ABOUT THE GREAT PRAIRIES OF ALCHEMILLAS AND HELICHRYSUMS, ABOUT THE ROCKY LEDGES CROWNED BY LOBELIAS TALLER THAN A MAN, AND ABOUT THE NUMBER OF RIVERS AND STREAMS WHICH GIVE RISE TO FORTY DIFFERENT WATERCOURSES, OF WHICH FOUR

INTRODUCTION The Green Infernos

ARE MAIN TRIBUTARIES OF THE NILE. MY FIRST CONTACT WITH THIS LAND HAPPENED AT NIGHT: FURTIVE FORMS OF ANTELOPES AND DUIKER CROSSED THE STONY TRAIL, OPENING THEIR BRIGHT EYES WIDE IN THE JEEP'S HEADLIGHTS. THE TRAIL RUNS ACROSS THE MIDDLE OF THE SANETTI PLATEAU, AT A HEIGHT OF ALMOST 13,000 FT (4000 M), AND ENDS AS IT ENTERS THE HARENNA FOREST WHICH, BETWEEN 9840 AND 3280 FT (3000 AND 1000 M), COVERS THE WHOLE SOUTHERN SLOPE OF THE MASSIF, BEFORE ENDING IN THE SCORCHING DESERT PLAIN.

APPROACHING FROM THE TOP, THE FIRST TREES THAT STAND OUT AMONG THE BUSHES ARE MONUMENTAL LICHEN-COVERED JUNIPERS, LOOKING LIKE CHRISTMAS

INTRODUCTION The Green Infernos

WREATHS. THE WOOD OF JUNIPERS GETS THICKER, NEXT TO THE CONIFERS LARGE HAGENIAS AND PODOCARPS APPEAR: IT TAKES MORE THAN THREE MEN TO HUG SOME OF THESE TRUNKS. THE MIST PASSES AMONG THE TREE TRUNKS, IT CONDENSES INTO TINY LITTLE DROPS COLLECTED BY THE EPIPHYTIC PLANTS, WHICH COVER THE BRANCHES AND TRUNKS LIKE A CARPET. THICK CLUMPS OF BAMBOO SHUT OFF THE VIEW, LIANAS AND TENDRILS JOIN THE TREES TOGETHER, CREATING A REALLY INTRICATE WEB. ON THE CROWN OF THE TREES COLOBUS MONKEYS RUN AFTER EACH OTHER, THE MALES LOOKING LIKE PATRIARCHS, THEIR FACES ADORNED BY A WHITE BEARD, USING THEIR LONG TAILS AS BALANCING POLES

The Green Infernos
Introduction

WHEN JUMPING ACROBATICALLY FROM BRANCH TO BRANCH. ONLY TINY FRACTION OF SUNLIGHT IS ABLE TO REACH THE UNDERGROWTH, WHICH IS INHABITED BY MANY CREATURES THAT HAVE FOUND REFUGE THERE, AWAY FROM THE SAVANNA AND THE BUSH, WHICH ARE OVERRUN BY MEN WHO SO FAR HAVE ALWAYS STAYED CLEAR OF THIS FABULOUS WORLD THAT FEEDS THE SPRINGS FROM WHICH RISE FORTY STREAMS. AMONG THEM ARE TWO OF THE HORN OF AFRICA'S MAIN RIVERS: THE JUBBA AND THE SHEBELI, WHICH FLOW TOWARD THE ARID REGIONS OF SOMALIA, WHOSE COAST IS WASHED BY THE WAVES OF THE INDIAN OCEAN.

- South America. Dendrobate frogs are widespread in tropical forests. They are also called "arrow frogs" because they're used by the Indians to poison the arrows they use for hunting.

Africa. A view of a mountain "cloud forest," a threatened habitat for the very rare gorilla sub-species.

Africa. Adult male mountain gorillas are also called "silverbacks" because of their characteristic coloring.

● Africa. A few thousand gorillas live in the Congo plain forests in Central Africa, but they are threatened by poaching and deforestation.

Africa. This episode of aggressiveness between gorillas is an isolated event that won't lead to combat. These animals much prefer peace to aggression.

152 • Africa. Most chameleons live on the island of Madagascar and in the rest of Eastern Africa; many of them are forest species.

153 • Africa. All macaques belong to the Macaca species. Their fur, which is thicker or thinner according to their environment, ranges in color from reddish brown to gray to dark brown.

154-155 • Africa. The Gabon viper's talent for perfect camouflage allows it to hide undetected in the underbrush of the African equatorial jungle.

156-157 ● Africa. The African lynx or caracal prefers dry areas on the border of dense vegetation.

157 ● Africa. The serval is an expert hunter of small roditors, and is widespread in most of Southern Africa and regions south of the Sahara.

Africa. Of all apes, the chimpanzee is the most versatile. Chimps discovered the advantages of living on the coast and in the mangrove swamps, which are full of crabs and other small prey.

160 • Africa. The chimpanzee uses small sticks to "fish" for ants and termites in the ground.

160-161 • Africa. A chimpanzee drinks from his cupped hand just like a human.

162 ● Africa. Mother and baby chimpanzee crossing a river full of dangerous crocodiles.

162-163 ● Africa. Chimpanzees are the most numerous group within the gorilla family. Even so, poaching threatens their long-term survival.

164 • Africa. A young chimpanzee
practicing climbing.

164-165 • Africa. The relationship
between adults and youngsters is very
intense and lasts for a number of years.

166 ● Africa. The mandrill, a relative of the baboon, is one of the most colorful African apes.

167 ● Africa. The baboon species, which conducts a gregarious existence in the forests of central western Africa, eats vegetables and small prey.

168-169 ● Africa. Forest elephants are smaller than savannah elephants; they also have smaller tusks.

169 ● Africa. Mother and youngster have just finished taking a mud bath in a forest clearing.

170 and 171 • Africa. Verreaux's lemurs is one of the most striking and vociferous species in Madagascar. These animals are at ease only when they are close to trees.

172-173 • Africa. A group of impalas is carefully observing the photographer as the animals decide whether to flee or to ignore the potential enemy.

180 ● South America. The caterpillar of a nocturnal butterfly shows off its surprising
camouflage tools.

181 ● Africa. These hymenopter larvas are well camouflaged in the leaves

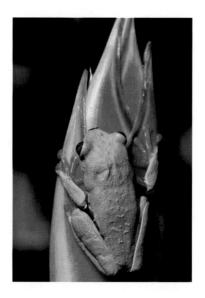

182 • South America. The skin of the Phyllomedusa (waxy frog) has obvious mimetic
qualities and it also secretes a chemical combination similar to an antibiotic.

183 • South America. Hummingbirds are widespread throughout both the American
continents but species are especially numerous near the equator.

● Asia. The douc langur is one of the rarest and most beautiful Asian monkeys. It feeds almost exclusively on leaves. It lives in groups of up to 10 members. The langur's appearance will differ according to age and habitat.

Asia. The orangutan can be as tall as a grown man. It has very long arm span (up to 8 ft/2.5 m), which helps it move easily through the dense jungles of the Far East.

188 • Asia. Orangutans are usually solitary and spend time with each other only during the mating season, but cubs remain with their mothers for a number of years.

189 • Asia. Their mothers teach young orangutans how to move through the forest and to search for food.

Asia. The future of the orangutan is a challenging issue. Deforestation continue to reduce its habitat, and poachers of adults and infants further endanger the species.

192 • Asia. Of all monkeys, the orangutan is the most comfortable in the tree-tops; it comes down only to drink or hunt for food. It's rare to see one wading through the monsoon-flooded jungle as in the photo.

193 • Asia. Orangutans are close relatives of man; they show this their human-like expressions and movements.

194 • Asia. The nasica is widespread on the island of Borneo, where it favors the forests, coastal mangroves and riverine woods.

195 • Asia. The nasica is an excellent climber. It owes its name to its well-developed nose. Prominent in males, it is considered to be a secondary sexual trait.

America. Monkeys in
the New World are
usually forest-dwellers.
The tamarin monkeys
are the most agile
ones. They feed on
leaves, shoots and fruit.

198 • Oceania. The koala is a tree-dwelling marsupial found only on the Australian continent.

198-199 • Oceania. The koala feeds only on certain types of eucalyptus leaves; it is able to digest them despite their oils and toxic substances.

South America. The jaguar is the largest and strongest American feline. Like its "cousin" the African leopard, it's an excellent climber and expert swimmer.

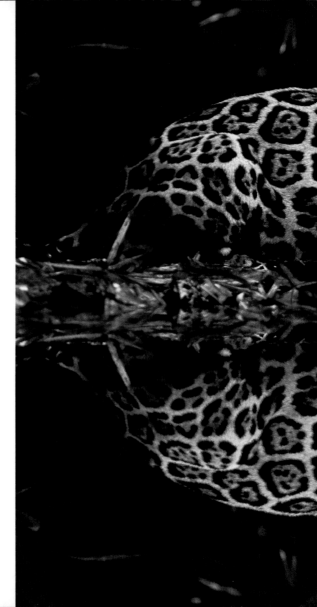

Asia. Leopards are
widespread thoughout
Africa and Asia . In Asia
they're called panthers.

208 and 209 • South America. The ocelot lives in the forests located between the two tropics. This solitary animal and excellent nocturnal hunter is about 3.2-ft (1-m) long. It spends its days in the dense forest.

210-211 • South America. Amongst the numerous species of anuria amphibians in the tropical forests, the leaf frog is particularly interesting because of its bright coloring.

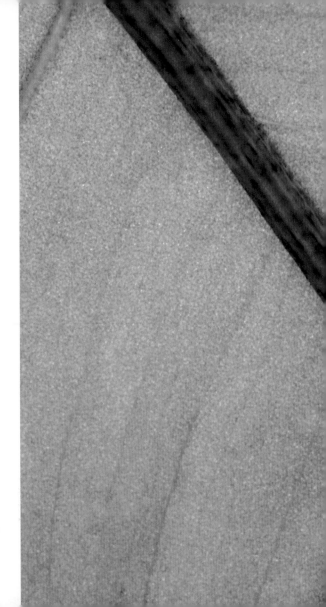

Africa. This tropical
tree frog leaning on a
leaf against the light is
also called a "glass
frog" because of
its transparent
"x-rayed" body.

214 • South America. This moth has bright mimetic coloring, which is unusual in nocturnal moths.

215 • South America. Transparent wings make this satiride butterfly almost invisible.

216-217 • South America. A flock of green-winged ara parrots crossing a clearing in the forest.

Asia. Komodo dragons are the largest lizards in the world weighing up to 220 lbs (100 kg), and growing toabout 9.8 ft (3 m) in lenght.

220 ● South America. Ara parrots bring their bright colors to the tropical and equatorial forests.

221 ● South America. Toucans have a large beak which they use to pick fruit and berries. Sometimes they eat the eggs and chicks of other birds.

222 • Africa. A tropical viper with its mouth open wide, is ready to attack. This is one of the world's most poisonous snakes.

223 • Africa. A leaf-tailed gecko opening its mouth, trying to scare off a predator.

224-225 • America. The liana serpent perfectly camouflages itself in trees by imitating the shape and arrangement of the tropical vines around it.

POLAR
HABITATS

COLIN MONTEATH

- North America. After birth, polar bear cubs live with their mother for two or three years until she mates again, which signals the start of the cubs' independence.

INTRODUCTION Polar Habitats

HUNTERS POLAR BEARS ARE. AN ICEBREAKER VOYAGE IS LIKELY TO COME UPON MORE BEARS OFF WRANGEL ISLAND, IN THE SIBERIAN ARCTIC. WHICH IS AN IMPORTANT BREEDING REGION, WHERE THE MOTHER BEARS MAKE THEIR DENS AND GIVE BIRTH. SADLY, POLAR BEARS ARE UNDER SIGNIFICANT THREAT FROM MAN-MADE CLIMATE CHANGE. ARCTIC SEA ICE IS SHRINKING DRAMATICALLY; THIS IN TURN AFFECTS THE MOVEMENT OF THE BEARS AND THEIR PREY OF SEALS AND WALRUSES. WALRUSES TOO ARE UNDER THREAT, IN PART BECAUSE OF POACHERS SEEKING THEIR IVORY TUSKS, WHICH WILL BE CARVED INTO SOUVENIRS. WALRUSES RANGE FROM SPITZBER-

INTRODUCTION Polar Habitats

GEN TO SIBERIA AND ALL THE WAY ACROSS THE ARC-
TIC BASIN TO ALASKA. THE INUIT HUNT THE WALRUS;
AS A RESULT WALRUSES ARE SHY CREATURES, OFTEN
DIFFICULT TO APPROACH AS THEY SUN THEMSELVES
ON ICE FLOES OR ON REMOTE ICE-FREE BEACHES.

POLAR BEARS, WALRUSES AND MANY OTHER ANIMALS
SUCH AS THE MUSK OX, ARCTIC FOX AND CARIBOU
ARE UNIQUE TO THE ARCTIC; THEY ARE NOT FOUND IN
ANTARCTICA. MANY OF THE BIRDS TOO, PUFFINS,
GUILLEMOTS, KITTIWAKES AND AUKS ARE ENDEMIC TO
THE ARCTIC, BUT ARE NOT VISITORS TO THE ANTARC-
TIC. THE TINY ARCTIC TERN, HOWEVER, FLIES ALL THE
WAY SOUTH TO ANTARCTICA FOR THE SOUTHERN

INTRODUCTION Polar Habitats

SUMMER, A VERY IMPRESSIVE PIECE OF NAVIGATION AND ENDURANCE.

THE EFFECTIVE SIZE OF ANTARCTICA DOUBLES EACH WINTER AS THE SOUTHERN OCEAN FREEZES. ITS DEEP COLD WATER FLOWS ALL THE WAY TO THE NORTHERN HEMISPHERE, AFFECTING WORLD WEATHER. SUCH COLD WATER ALSO SUPPORTS THE GREATEST NUMBER OF PLANT AND ANIMAL SPECIES, MUCH RICHER THAN TROPICAL REGIONS. ANTARCTICA DOESN'T HAVE MANY SPECIES BUT THOSE THAT ARE THERE, FROM THE TINY ZOO- AND PHYTO-PLANKTON TO THE LARGER CREATURES SUCH AS PENGUINS AND SEALS, EXIST IN GREAT NUMBERS.

INTRODUCTION Polar Habitats

ANTARCTICA IS WELL KNOWN AS THE HIGHEST, DRIEST, COLDEST AND WINDIEST CONTINENT. ONLY 2 PERCENT OF THE CONTINENT IS ICE-FREE. HOWEVER, ALMOST ALL OF ITS WILDLIFE LIVES AROUND THE COASTAL FRINGE, WRESTING A LIVING FROM THE SEA. PENGUINS ARE ANTARCTICA'S STAR ATTRACTION. THE ONLY TRULY ANTARCTIC PENGUINS ARE THE ADÉLIE AND THE EMPEROR, THE LARGEST AND MOST SOUTHERLY OF ALL PENGUINS. MOST PENGUIN SPECIES SUCH AS THE KING, GENTOO, MAGELLANIC, YELLOW-EYED, ROYAL AND NUMEROUS CRESTED PENGUINS LIVE ON SUB-ANTARCTIC ISLANDS SOUTH OF NEW ZEALAND, AUSTRALIA, SOUTH AFRICA, TIERRA

DEL FUEGO AND ON THE REMOTE ISLAND OF SOUTH GEORGIA.

THE EMPEROR PENGUIN'S LIFE CYCLE IS TRULY AMAZING. THE FEMALE LAYS THE EGG IN MID-WINTER ON THE SEA ICE; THE MALE INCUBATES IT UNDER A FLAP OF FEATHERS ABOVE HIS FEET FOR MANY DARK MONTHS UNTIL THE FEMALE RETURNS WITH FOOD. LIVING OFF THEIR RESERVES OF BODY FAT, THE MALES STAY WARM BY FORMING LARGE, CONTINUALLY MOVING "HUDDLES" WITH HUNDREDS OF OTHER MALES, ALL TRYING TO BALANCE THEIR PRECIOUS EGG ON THEIR FEET.

THE MOST NUMEROUS MAMMAL ON EARTH IS THE

● North America. A group of polar bears about to feed on a whale carcass that ocean currents carried to this bay in Alaska. Large stomachs enable bear to eat huge quantities of food – and to go for months without eating when it is hard to catch prey.

240 and 241 ● North America. Male polar bears fight bloody battles during the mating season. Few females are free to mate free to mate; most are busy raising their offspring.

242-243 ● North America. Both cubs and adult polar bears like to play. Here, these two Canadian bears are pretending to fight.

244 • North America. Polar bears often spend time playing together, especially during the good season when food is abundant.

245 • North America. This polar bear seems to be showing off for the camera. Bears are rather solitary animals and very good hunters, but they are also unexpectedly playful.

● North America. This Canadian polar bear is lying on its stomach, resting. It's alone because polar bears generally prefer a solitary life except during the mating season and when they are raising their young.

248 left • North America. Polar bears have very thick fur which protects them from the cold. They don't even need to find shelter during snow storms; they just lie down in the snow to reduce the amount of body surface exposed to the cold.

248 right and 249 • North America. Polar bears often strike funny poses, showing unexpected agility for animals of their size.

250-251 • North America. Polar bear cubs live with their mother for two or three years before moving away. Then, it will take them two more years to reach sexual maturity.

252-253 • North America. A group of polar bears in the polar sunset waiting for night to fall.

North America. Two Artic foxes are playing on a Canadian beach. We can tell that it's summer because their fur is brown and not white.

North America. The walrus is a lazy animal and spends much time resting on the pack ice. The ones in the photo have long fangs and "moustaches" which help them to find the shellfish they love to eat.

North America. Walruses lying on a pebbly Alaskan beach off the Bering Sea. They use their enormous upper canines during fights and as pivots to help them climb out of the water and onto the pack ice.

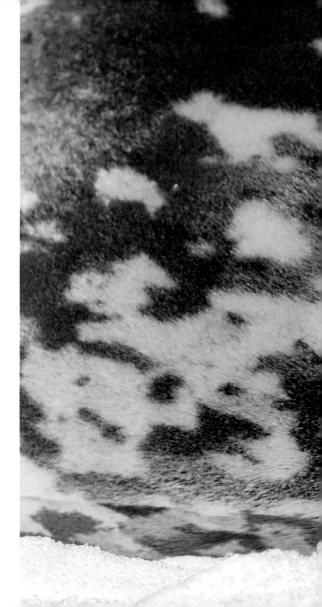

North America. Their spotted coats and large size distinguish adult Greenland seals from their cubs. These cubs (unfortunately!) have a splendid white fur which is very much sought after.

● North America. This Greenland seal cub is resting near its mother on pack ice on the Canadian island of La Madeleine. Seal cubs are exposed to many risks; they include being hunted by humans for their fur and being attacked by various predators.

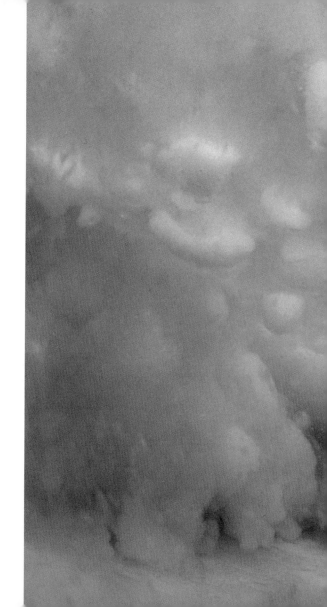

● North America. Even though it's very young, this Greenland seal cub is easily swimming under the pack ice near La Madeleine island.

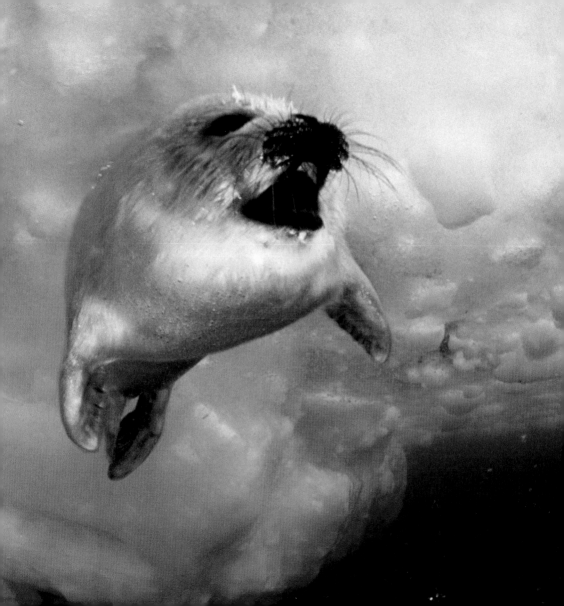

● North America. The beluga whale, also called the white dolphin, has a round, protruding forehead and waxy skin which is dark gray in young belugas. Belugas are still hunted today for their skin, which makes a very strong leather.

268 and 269 ● North America. The killer whale is found in all the cold seas of the world. Many of them live in the icy waters of the North Pole where, in the summer, they hunt fish, squid, dolphins, seals, sea lions and penguins.

270-271 ● South America. A black-eyebrow albatross, taking care of its chick on the Falkland Islands.

272 and 273 • Oceania. Crested penguins(a macaron on the left and a rockhopper on the right) build their nests on the islands close to Antarctica and on the Australian coast, Tasmania, and New Zealand. Here, we see them during mating season when they are most prone to conflict.

274-275 • Antarctica. The photo shows a papua penguin expertly "surfing" the ocean waves.

276 • South America. Male and female royal penguins take turns incubating their eggs. Here, we see them on the Falkland Islands, located in the southernmost part of the Atlantic Ocean.

277 • Oceania. We are prone to "humanize" royal penguins because of their upright posture and cute gestures.

278 • South America. A papua penguin, in a bizarre position, is scratching its head with a flipper.

279 • Antarctica. Also known as the Antarctic *pigoscelide* or chinstrap, this penguin boasts mask-like markings around its face.

280 • Antarctica. Three Adélie penguins diving off an iceberg in the waters of the Antarctic circle.

281 • Antarctica. An Emperor penguin gets out of the water in favor of the pack ice in the Weddell Sea.

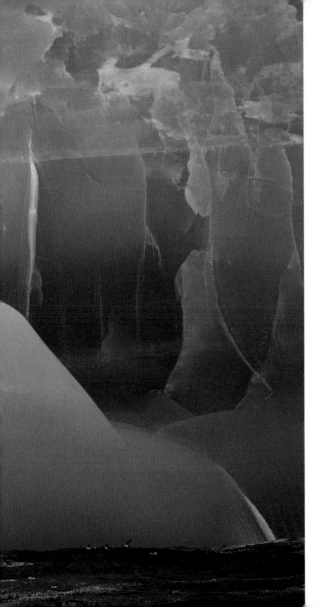

● Antarctica. A group
of chinstrap penguins
resting on a magnificent
blue-colored iceberg.

● Oceania. A group of emperor penguins swimming under the pack ice: their short wings, unsuitable for flight, make wonderful flippers in underwater.

Antarctica. Leopard seals look gentle but they are actually fearful predators and can grow to a length of 13 ft (4 m) and a weight of 1100 lbs (500 kg). The owe their name to the spots on their backs and fronts.

Antarctica. A leopard seal captures an Adélie penguin which is too small to defend itself.

● Antarctica. Emperor
penguins trying to
protect themselves
from the icy wind by
positioning themselves
in a circle.

292 and 293 • Antarctica. This newborn emperor penguin seeks shelter close to its mother. When it gets hungry, it sounds a shrill cry and its mother (right) regurgitates food for it.

294-295 • Antarctica. Like children awaiting their turns, Adélie penguins dive off this beautiful blue iceberg one at a time and seem to be having fun while preparing to hunt for food.

LIFE

amid the

DUNES

CRISTINA MARIA BANFI

- Africa. The sun is low on the horizon and a solitary oryx moves between the red dunes of the Namib desert. The dunes can rise to about 1000 ft (300 m) high.

INTRODUCTION Life Amid the Dune

My FIRST VIEW, EARLY ONE MORNING, OF THE VAST SAHARA DESERT: AN ENDLESS SEA OF GOLDEN SAND, SILENT AND WILD. THE EYE LOSES ITS POINT OF REFERENCE AND MAGIC RULES: THESE ARE THE MEMORIES THAT REMAIN MOST VIVID IN THE MIND.

ALL AROUND, LOW PORPHYRY HILLS RISE LIKE LOST ISLANDS REFLECTING THE RAYS OF A HOT SUN STILL UNABLE TO SCORCH THE ROCKS. THE FARTHEST LANDSCAPES LOOK PECULIARLY CROOKED OWING TO THE DRY AIR – AND HAVE REMAINED SO FOR MILLENNIA, SOME SAY WAITING FOR A "MIRACULOUS REAWAKENING."

SEEMINGLY NOTHING MOVED AS I EXPLORED MY DESERT REGION DURING MY DAYS THERE. YET THE APPARENT INACTIVITY

INTRODUCTION Life Amid the Dune

HIDES A RICH VARIETY OF LIVING CREATURES, WHICH THRIVE IN THE DARK. WATER SHORTAGE HERE, MORE THAN ANYWHE-RE ELSE, MAKES THE STRUGGLE FOR SURVIVAL CRUELLER AND HARDER. DURING THE DAYTIME THE SMALL EGYPTIAN GERBILS WAIT PATIENTLY IN THEIR HOLES IN THE SAND FOR THE COOLNESS OF THE NIGHT, AS DOES THE AGILE LARGE-EA-RED FENNEC FOX. ON THE GROUND A FEW SIGNS REVEAL THE PRESENCE OF A ROUGH-SCALED SNAKE THAT IS HIDING CAU-TIOUSLY UNDER A FEW INCHES OF SAND.

I'M AMAZED TO THINK ABOUT THE EXTRAORDINARY METABO-LISM OF DESERT ANIMALS, SPECIALIZED IN SAVING EVERY SIN-GLE DROP OF PRECIOUS WATER. THE LETHAL STINGING SCOR-PION AND SMALL BEETLES ARE PROTECTED BY LEATHERY CU-

Life Amid the Dune

Introduction

TICLE THAT RETAINS THE BODY'S MOISTURE, WHILE OTHER ANIMALS ARE ABLE TO SURVIVE WITHOUT EVER DRINKING. I WATCH THE HORIZON AND I KNOW FOR SURE THAT ON A GIVEN NIGHT, AS ON EVERY OTHER NIGHT, THE STRUGGLE FOR SURVIVAL BETWEEN PREDATOR AND PREY WILL TAKE PLACE. HESITATINGLY I SCOOPED UP A HANDFUL OF SAND AND FELT THE THRILL OF POSSESSION. IT WAS SHORT LIVED: WITHIN SECONDS THE LIGHT GRAINS HAD SLIPPED THROUGH MY FINGERS AND WERE CARRIED AWAY BY THE WIND AND SETTLED ELSEWHERE ON THE DESERT. NOW I SEE IN THE DESERT THE SENSE OF FREEDOM, THAT SAME FREEDOM WHICH MAKES THE TUAREG THE FASCINATING LORDS OF THE DESERT.

- Africa. The special scales on the sides of its body enable the ceraste viper to wriggle quickly back and forth and hide under the blazing sand.

Africa. A small Cape fox is peacefully napping. It's waiting for the right time to start hunting its prey, which sometimes includes young lambs.

304 and 305 • Africa. Two fennecs exchanging tender gestures. These small foxes with their bat-like ears are usually monogamous. They live in family groups, share the same den, and cooperate when hunting or defending themselves.

306-307 • Africa. A rare albino dromedary amid very sparse vegetation. These animals can close their nostrils at will to keep out the sand.

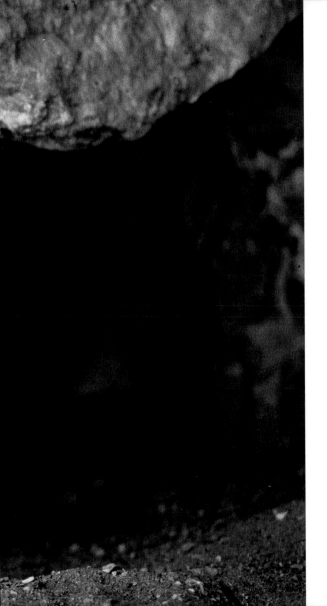

Africa. A rocky hollow provides the caracal with a cool place to spend the hottest hours of the day while waiting to begin to hunt when night falls.

312 • Africa. A sand cat expertly confronting its prey, ready to launch its final attack. These felines are excellent snake hunters.

313 • Africa. Sand cats can live in the dessert without having to drink; they get the liquids they need from their food.

314-315 • Africa. A terrifying sight in the sand, this viper, its mouth open wide, will soon sink its poisonous fangs into its prey.

316-317 • Africa. A group of gemsbok in the hot sun, studying the horizon. These groups usually have 25 to 30 members, often mainly females with their offspring.

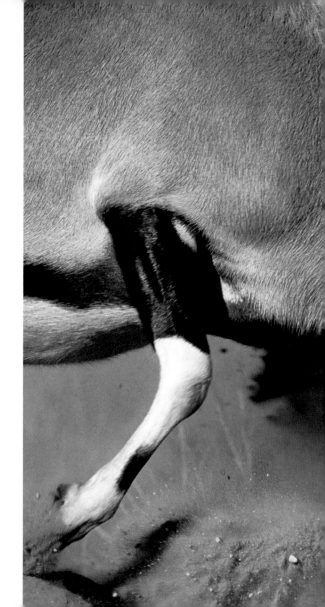

Africa. These two male gemsbok are fighting, using their long, strong horns as weapons. Dominance for this species is based on age and size.

Africa. A group of ostriches strolling between high sand dunes in the Namib desert, which has some of the highest dunes in the world.

322 ● Africa. Like all mammal cubs, young suricates spend a great deal of time playing together, consolidating relationships within the colony.

323 ● Africa. An affectionate adult taking care of some defenseless chicks. Male ostriches play the primary role in protecting and raising the chicks.

324 • Africa. An adult carefully carries a newborn. Both parents share responsibility for care
of the young together with all the adult members of the colony.

325 • Africa. Two suricates outside their underground den, warming themselves
in the sun, standing up on their hind legs. This position helps them to watch for
potential danger.

326-327 • Africa. Are these two lionesses getting so close to this porcupine because of hunger or because of curiosity?

327 • Africa. Discouraged by these sharp needles, even the strongest predator gives up.

328 • Africa. This duel, fought to establish individual rank within the group by force, raises clouds of dust.

329 • Africa. It's best to run away when the situation looks bad. Paws armed with sharp claws are dangerous weapons. Claws are also used for digging.

330-331 • Africa. A herd of antelopes leaping away in compact group formation. An antelope herd might be comprised of even a thousand members, and the bigger the herd, the more protection it affords.

North America. A puma prowls on a high ridge overlooking the landscape of the canyons. This solitary feline is able to survive even in harsh environments like the desert.

336 • North America. Puma cubs learning to run and fight. At birth, they have spotted red fur whic; thish changes to a solid color with age maturity.

337 • North America. A running puma displays the gracefulness and agility characteristic of all felines. Its fur is the same color as the sand.

● North America. Pumas are also called mountain lions; they can move easily even over steep and difficult terrain.

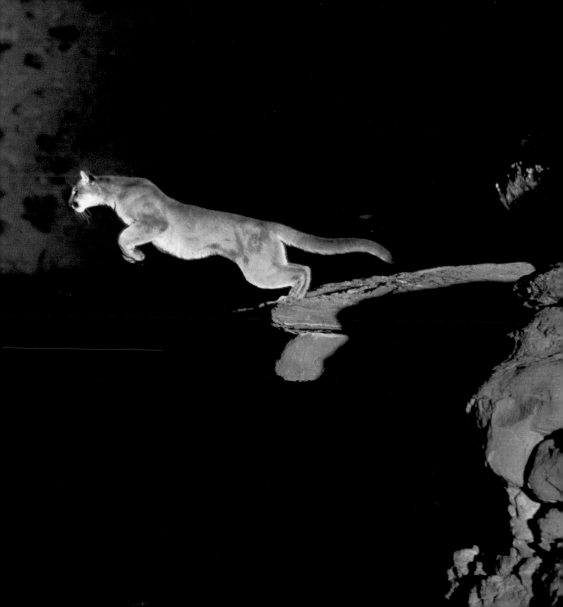

340 • North America. A thorny cactus can make a comfortable and safe nest. This Harris vulture won't have to fear for her chicks.

341 • North America. A large cactus owl and its chick are exchanging tender gestures. The mother is waiting for night to begin her hunting.

● South America. The slopes of the Andes, even though rather bare, provide food and shelter to a family of guanacos, comprised of a male and several females.

344 • Oceania. The dry desert expanses of the Australian interior are home to these kangaroos, the largest marsupials in the world.

345 • Oceania. A young kangaroo looks out of its mother's comfortable pouch with curiosity and a bit of fear.

Oceania. An emu racing through the red rocks of the Australian desert. Even though this bird is able to fly, it's a fast runner and can reach a speed of up to 30 mph (50 kph).

348 • Oceania. A small gecko in Queensland has come out of its den in search of food; it is entrusting its safety from predators to its mimetic coloring.

349 • Oceania. Just a few drops of rain are all that's needed to waken this Spencer frog which had buried itself in the sand to survive the dry period.

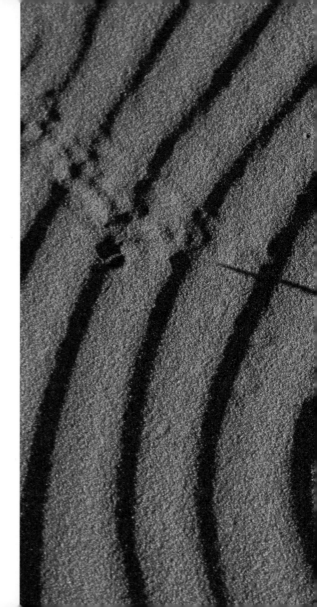

Oceania. A moloch, a thorny lizard with mimetic coloring, erases the tracks the wind has left in the Australian desert sand.

The GREAT BLUE

ALBERTO LUCA RECCHI

- Indian Ocean. The great white shark, which is at the top of the food chain, puts a great deal of energy into its attacks (here, we can't see its prey).

The Great Blue

Introduction

ABOUT THE SEA WE KNOW VERY LITTLE. MY GENERATION IS ONLY THE SECOND TO GO DIVING. THERE HAVE BEEN MORE PEOPLE ON THE MOON, AS MANY AS ELEVEN IN THE APOLLO MISSIONS, THAN IN THE SEA'S GREATEST DEPTHS. JUST TWO OF SCIENTISTS, 40 YEARS AGO, WITH THE BATHYSCAPHE *TRIESTE*. EVEN WHEN WE WEAR DIVING MASKS AND SWIM UNDERWATER WE CAN SEE VERY LITTLE, JUST ABOUT 65 FT (20 M). THUS, IF A WHALE HAD TO TURN ITS HEAD, IT WOULD NOT BE ABLE TO SEE ITS TAIL.

YET, IF EVER THERE WAS A REALM OF PREDATORS, THE SEA IS IT. THE BASE OF THE FOOD PYRAMID, MARINE PLANTS AND HERBIVORES, IS MADE ALMOST ENTIRELY OF MICROSCOPIC ORGANISMS OF PLANKTON. PRACTICALLY NO FISH GRAZE,

• Pacific Ocean. A humpback whale followed by its calf, which was more than 13 ft (4 m) long at birth and weighed almost a ton (1000 kg).

INTRODUCTION The Great Blue

THEY ARE ALL HUNTERS. IT CAN'T BE EASY FOR THEM TO RE-LAX. CHASES AND AMBUSHES FOLLOW ONE AFTER ANOTHER, INCESSANTLY. TO AVOID ENDING UP AS SOMEBODY ELSE'S MEAL A FISH NEEDS TO BE CONSTANTLY ALERT, READY TO FIGHT OR SWIM AWAY. OR ELSE TO CAMOUFLAGE ITSELF, WHICH REQUIRES A GOOD DOSE OF BRAVERY. KILLING IS THE RULE. SPERM WHALES, TUNA AND BARRACUDAS KILL, BUT SO DO PILCHARDS AND SOLES. THE TRICKS OF HUNTING AMONG SEA-DWELLERS ARE EVERY BIT AS GOOD AS THOSE OF THE SAVANNA'S FAUNA. THE ONLY DIFFERENCES ARE THE TEETH AND THE DIMENSIONS OF SCALE. "BIG FISH EAT LITTLE FISH" IS NOT A COMMONPLACE, IT IS DAILY LIFE.

ALMOST EVERYBODY TENDS TO STAND UP FOR THE LITTLE FISH, THE LOSER. A MOUTH ARMED WITH A TRAP BRISTLING

INTRODUCTION The Great Blue

WITH TEETH IS NOT GOING TO BE POPULAR. THE SHARK KNOWS THIS. IF EVER ANY CREATURE WAS CUT OUT FOR THE ROLE OF UNPLEASANT FELLOW, HE IS THE ONE. BUT I CONFESS, I'M ON HIS SIDE. IN FACT, I'VE BEEN MEETING THEM THROUGHOUT MY LIFE. I LOOK FOR THEM FOR MY WORK: TO TAKE PICTURES OF THEM AND TO FILM THEM. HOW MANY I'VE MET I CAN'T REMEMBER; I'VE KEPT COUNT ONLY FOR THE WHITE SHARK. MORE THAN 50 TIMES HIS BLACK EYE, AS BIG AS A PING-PONG BALL, HAS MET MINE, AND EVERY TIME WAS DIFFERENT. I KNOW HE WOULDN'T HESITATE FOR A MOMENT TO BITE CLEAN THROUGH ME, AND MAYBE THIS TOO IS WHY I AM FASCINATED BY HIM.IN MY OWN WAY, I'M A "VICTIM" MYSELF – EVEN IF NO SHARK HAS YET USED HIS TEETH ON ME. IT ALL STARTED WITH MY FIRST MEETING WITH A WHITE SHARK.

INTRODUCTION The Great Blue

A CHANCE ENCOUNTER. I WAS ON THE OTHER SIDE OF THE WORLD LOOKING FOR SPINY LOBSTERS. A DIVE JUST LIKE ANY OTHER, BROWSING AMONG THE SUNKEN ROCKS. FINALLY I FOUND ONE, DIPPED MY ARM TO THE BOTTOM OF THE LAIR TO GET IT OUT, WHEN I FELT A PRESENCE BEHIND ME. SILENT, BUT HUGE. YES, BECAUSE THE SHARK DOESN'T GROWL, HE DOESN'T ROAR, HE ARRIVES SILENTLY. I TURNED AROUND AND MY ARM GOT STUCK IN THE ROCK. I TURNED MY HEAD AND SAW A HUGE HEAD A FEW FEET AWAY FROM ME, A HALF-OPEN MOUTH, THE TEETH PROTRUDING.

BY INSTINCT I DID A STUPID THING, I PULLED MY ARM FREE FROM THE ROCK, BUT I CUT MYSELF AND MY ARM STARTED BLEEDING. I THOUGHT: THIS IS THE END. I LIVED THOSE MOMENTS AS IF THEY WERE MY LAST, AND YET THE MOST UN-

INTRODUCTION The Great Blue

LIKELY THING HAPPENED. WITHIN A HAIR'S BREADTH OF ME THE SHARK TURNED, SWAM ALONGSIDE ME AND CONTINUED ON HIS PATROL WITHOUT EVEN DEIGNING TO SO MUCH AS LOOK AT ME. IN SHORT, I WAS REPRIEVED. MAYBE I JUST FELT GRATITUDE.

TO MEET ONE, THOUGH, IS NOT EASY, IN ADDITION BECAUSE THERE AREN'T MANY LEFT. THE PREDATOR WITH A CAPITAL "P", WHO IS US HUMANS, IS WIPING THE SHARKS OUT FOR NOTHING IN PARTICULAR: TO STEAL THEIR FINS, WHICH IN MANY ASIAN COUNTRIES COOKS USE FOR MAKING SOUP, OR BECAUSE THEY END UP IN FISH-NETS MEANT FOR OTHER FISH. FINDING THE GREAT WHITE SHARK IS GETTING MORE AND MORE DIFFICULT, THOUGH HE KNOWS HOW TO COPE FOR SURE. A FEW YEARS AGO I SPENT SIX MONTHS AROUND THE

The Great Blue

MEDITERRANEAN, HOPING TO MEET ONE. STILL, IT'S IN THESE WATERS THAT THE LARGEST SHARK KNOWN TO MEN HAS BEEN CAUGHT; ALMOST 23 FT (7 M) IN LENGTH.

NO, I'M NO DOOMSTER. AT THE TOP OF THE FOOD PYRAMID, SHARKS HAVE BEEN THE DIRECTORS OF THE GREAT EAT AND GOT TO EAT GAME FOR 240 MILLION YEARS. WE'RE NOT THE ONES WHO'LL SUPERSEDE THEM. BECAUSE THE SEA IS MUCH BIGGER AND MUCH LESS KNOWN THAN WE IMAGINE. MORE-OVER, HOW GOOD LIFE IS, AND WHAT A PRIVILEGE TO DO THIS JOB OF DIVING, TO WITNESS GREAT SPECTACLES OF THE DEEP THAT MAY NEVER HAVE BEEN SEEN BEFORE. I HOPE TO CON-TINUE DOING IT UNTIL I'M EIGHTY. HAPPY DIVING EVERYBODY!

361 • Indian Ocean. In the sea, it isn't always a "dog-eat-dog" life: this shy clownfish, for example, is letting itself be defended by the anemone's stinging tentacles .

362-363 • Pacific Ocean. Bottlenose dolphins live in groups with 10 to 20 members.

Atlantic Ocean. The albatross (the one in the photo has black eyebrows) is a very efficient flyer. It saves energy by masterfully exploiting air currents.

366 • Atlantic Ocean. The American pelican catches fish by taking short dives or even by swimming.

366-367 • Pacific Ocean. The comparison with a sea gull shows how big the Australian pelican is: it is the largest bird in the world and has a wing span of 11.5 ft (3.5 m).

● Mediterranean Sea. The herring gull weighs less than a
2.2 lbs (1 kg). Here, a young one (recognizable by its
spotted feathers) is practicing flying over the sea.

Atlantic Ocean.
Whether on land or sea,
the bald eagle almost
always catches its prey.

372 • Atlantic Ocean. Spotted dolphins are very happy when they're together in a group.

373 • Atlantic Ocean. Spotted dolphins surfacing in search of fish or squid.

Indian Ocean. A group of dolphins hunting in a school of sardines, this fish is one of their favorite foods.

376 • Atlantic Ocean. The spotted dolphin has an agile and slender body and may live up to 40 years.

377 • Atlantic Ocean. A spotted dolphin opening its mouth which has 80 pair of very sharp pointed teeth.

378-379 • Red Sea. A bottlenose dolphin playing cat and mouse with an octopus.

Atlantic Ocean. Common dolphins are rather voracious. They have to eat a great deal of food to maintain their weight which may exceed 285 lbs (130 kg).

Atlantic Ocean. The shark has been lord of the sea for millions of years. It is so successful in evolutionary terms that nature has yet to create anything more efficient.

● Atlantic Ocean. On opposite shores of the Atlantic Ocean, two great white sharks are proving their strength. Their feeding, however, isn't blindly voracious; they are sometimes rather cautious and they feed relatively rarely.

● Atlantic Ocean. The sand tiger shark, which has a very scary appearance, is actually quite peaceful.

● Pacific Ocean. Sharks also hunt
their prey on the surface of the
water as the albatross on the left
is learning; the albatross on the
right didn't have a chance to learn.

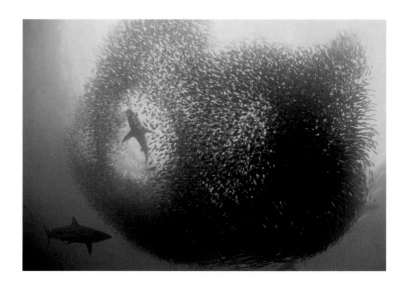

392 • Atlantic Ocean. Schools of fish escaping predators create bizarre shapes as shown here, where thousands of sardines are fleeing from a copper shark.

393 • Indian Ocean. A copper shark bursting into a school of sardines and scattering them.

394 • Pacific Ocean. The hammerhead is one of the most efficient predators of the seas. During the day, hammerhead sometimes form large groups but, at night, they hunts alone.

394-395 • Pacific Ocean. The hammerhead's bizarre head acts as an efficient radar which picks up all the conditions in the water.

● Pacific Ocean. One of the most exciting sights in the sea is the sudden surfacing of a group of humpback whales; each whale might weigh up to 40 tons (40,500 kg).

398 • Pacific Ocean. The movements of these humpback whales might be connected to mating rituals or they might just be having fun.

399 • Pacific Ocean. The Latin name of the humpback whale (*megattera*) means "big wings" and refers to the front fins (which might be even 16.5 ft/5 m long) of these extraordinary mammals which appear to be flying when they swim.

● Pacific Ocean. Even though it seems impossible for animals 50 ft (15 m) long to do so, when these humpback whales leap they raise their bodies completely out of the water.

402 • Pacific Ocean. The long folds under the large "face" of the humpback whale enable it to increase its volume and be able to eat a greater quantity of plankton.

403 • Pacific Ocean. The protuberances on the head of the humpback whale contain stiff hairs which may register tactile sensations.

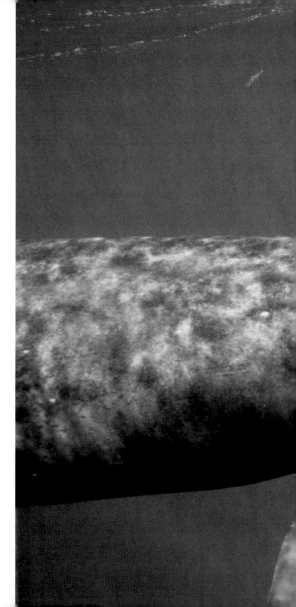

Pacific Ocean. Infant humpback whales are 10 to 13 ft ((3 to 4 m) long at birth and need to be nourished with almost 110 lbs (50 kg) of milk every day.

● Atlantic Ocean. The black right whale (left, a female with her calf) lives only in the cold waters of the southern hemisphere. The protrusions of hard skin on the their heads are a means of identifying individual whales.

408 • Pacific Ocean. A sperm whale diving. This cetacean can hunt at a depth greater than 3280 to 6560 ft (1000 to 2000 m).

408-409 • Indian Ocean. Bryde's whales feed on krill along with fish, including sardines, and, seemingly, small sharks.

● Atlantic Ocean. Sperm whales live in groups with varying numbers ranging from about twenty to several hundred. The mother cares for the young for only two years even though they don't reach maturity until 18 to 20!

Atlantic Ocean. The
brown pelican is a
solitary hunter which
takes spectacular dives
into the sea.

Atlantic Ocean. The brown pelican on the right looks as if it's making a sound, but these birds are mute when they become adults.

North Sea. A pair of puffins are on top of a rock on Norway's northern coast. These birds don't build nests but, instead, take shelter in actual dens.

420 • North Sea. A female gray seal refuses the attentions of a male.

421 • Pacific Ocean. Among elephant seals, the battle for rank is violent. Few of these animals are able to win the right to mate and this makes the loser males even more aggressive.

Pacific and Atlantic Oceans. The relationship between mother sea lions and their young is a very tender one (left, New Zealand sea lions and right, South American ones).

424 • Atlantic Ocean. This cacique cleaner bird doesn't have to worry about waking this elephant seal because, though these seals are usually grumpy, they appreciate its services.

425 • Pacific Ocean. This elephant seal can relax. Even though this species was hunted almost to extermination in the 19th century, the seals are no longer hunted at all.

426 • Pacific Ocean. The mother-child relationship for the eared seals (or sea lions) of New Zealand is one of the closest and most affectionate ones of all finned creatures.

426-427 • Pacific Ocean. Eared seal (or sea lion) females of the Galapagos Islands give birth to only one pup at a time, and then spend three years raising it.

Sea of Cortez. Noisy colonies of California seals, comprised of numerous members, and flocks of white pelicans share one of the world's most beautiful natural environments.

● Atlantic Ocean. Killer whales, with their 5-ton (5080-kg) weight, will willingly beach themselves to attack a group of unlucky eared seal cubs, using a terrifying hunting technique.

Atlantic Ocean. Killer whales leap in a spectacular way either to show off their dominant status or to better observe their surroundings.

Pacific Ocean. The grampus or killer whale actually forms an extended family, and the adults teach their skills to the newborn. New mothers, too, learn how to raise their young from the more experienced females.

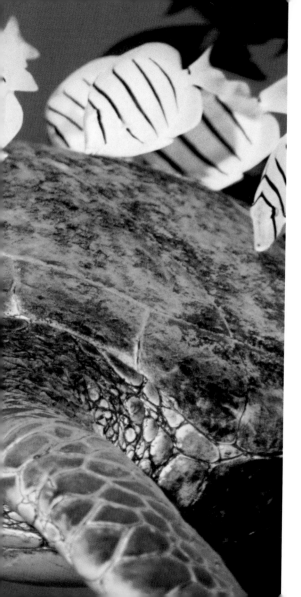

438-439 ● Pacific Ocean. Like many other sea creatures, the green turtle, too, willingly accepts the services of "cleaners," in this case the *acanthurus fish*, which frees it of algae and parasites.

439 ● Indian Ocean. The head of this hawksbill turtle has a robust beak; it resembles that of a parrot.

440-441 ● Atlantic Ocean. The ray's mouth is on its ventral side. These cartilaginous fish are very ancient. Here, we see one exploring the sand in search of food.

442-443 ● Pacific Ocean. Though barracudas are generally solitary, they sometimes form small schools especially when they are young.

444 • Indian Ocean. Having different diets, manta rays and barracudas don't compete for food.

445 • Red Sea. The carangids are voracious predators and live by the hundreds in schools.

446-447 • Indian Ocean. The green turtle is usually found in shallow water near the coast even though it's capable of crossing the oceans if migrating.

● Pacific Ocean. The manta ray
has a large mouth with lamina able
to filter plankton. It lives in the
warm tropical waters near coral
reefs.

● Pacific Ocean. These "flocks" of numerous Munk's manta devil rays are a wonderful sight.

452 • Pacific Ocean. Two suckerfish are holding on to the lobes of a manta ray and are getting a free ride.

453 • Pacific Ocean. Manta rays are sociable animals with a complex intelligence.

Pacific Ocean. Some manta rays, probably performing a mating dance, swimming near a coral reef.

Pacific Ocean. The daytime octopus is hard to see when it's on the seabed, but its normal color stands out when it's surrounded by water.

Indian Ocean. The clownfish often chooses a magnificent anemone to be its fortress and provide it and its eggs with protection.

468 • Pacific Ocean. The broken rocks of the coral reef are yellow moray eels' favorite place. Here, they can easily ambush their prey and satisfy their intense curiosity.

469 • Pacific Ocean. The lion fish swims in a slow and stately manner.

Indian Ocean. The butterfly fish is one of the most colorful tropical fish. It's present in 11 genres and 127 varieties.

472 • Pacific Ocean. A cup-shaped coral devouring a small cephalopod.

473 • Atlantic Ocean. The nurse shark isn't as gentle as its name implies when dealing with the fish of the reef.

474-475 • Indian Ocean. Butterfly fish explore the reef looking for plankton.

● Indian Ocean. Yellow tail fins signal the passage of a school of fusilier fish hunting for plankton near a coral reef.

• Pacific Ocean. Local iguanas and red rock crabs share the bare crags of the Galapagos Islands. Even though oceans cover an enormous surface area of the globe, nowhere else except here did evolution stopped millions of years ago.

Pacific Ocean. A Galapagos sea lion is playing with an unfortunate pufferfish (left) while a Steller sea lion is playing with a starfish. Sea lions love to play and they are very curios about everything they see. This strong curiosity, however, can get them into trouble when they come across man-made objects and debris.

482 • Pacific Ocean. Sea lions are very sociable animals as shown by this group of young ones on a shoal in the Galapagos.

483 • Pacific Ocean. Sea lions are excellent swimmers. It even looks as if they are surfing the whitecaps. They hunt herring, mackerel, cephalopods and even small sharks.

484 and 485 • Pacific Ocean. Sea lions are perfectly adapted to life in the sea. They can shut their nostrils underwater, and have big eyes to see in the dim underwater light. They also have a great deal of subcutaneous fat to keep them warm, and powerful fins for swimming.

486-487 • Pacific Ocean. The Galapagos penguin doesn't like the heat so it swims in the cold Cromwell current to cool off and to hunt for prey.

LIFE

on the

PRAIRIES

ANGELA SERENA ILDOS

- North America. A male elk coming out of a pool. This majestic species of deer is perfectly at ease in the water; it is a source of food and protection for them.

INTRODUCTION Life on the Prairies

A SUCCESSION OF SILVER WAVES ON THE EMER-
ALD SURFACE ENGAGES THE VIEW AS FAR AS THE EYE CAN
SEE. SUDDENLY, A DASH OF LIFE, A FLASH OF GREY. A USU-
ALLY SHY CREATURE, PERHAPS INTRIGUED BY THE ANOMALY
OF MY CURIOUS HUMAN PRESENCE, DARES TO RAISE ITS
HEAD OVER THIS LIMITLESS SEA; ONE MEET THE DREAMY
EYES OF A RHEA. THE ENDLESS PAMPAS; THIS IS THE SEA I
LOVE TALKING ABOUT. IT'S THE ONLY TOPIC THAT LETS ONE
KEEP ONE'S FEET ON THE GROUND. AND WHAT A GROUND! I
LOVE THE STRONG SWEETNESS OF THESE MOORS, WHERE
THE WIND NEVER ABATES, BLOWING FARAWAY SCENTS AND
SOUNDS COLORED BY THE GAUCHOS' IMAGINATION. AND
ABOVE ALL I LOVE ITS ANIMALS. THE ARMADILLO'S APPAR-
ENT CLUMSINESS – HERE CALLED PELUDO, SO ECCENTRIC

INTRODUCTION Life on the Prairies

AND CUTE, HE IS SURE TO PUT UP WITH THE ADVERSITIES OF THE WORLD, PROTECTED ONLY BY HIS HAIRY ARMOR. THE NEST-BUILDING EFFORT OF THE OVENBIRD, THE SOFTNESS OF THE VISCACHA'S FUR, THAT ONE COULD TOUCH WITH ONE'S EYES EVEN BEFORE ONE'S HANDS. A PRAIRIE MILLIONS OF YEARS OLD, BUT WHERE EVERY STEM IS NOT MORE THAN A FEW WEEKS OLD. PLANTS GROW QUICKLY, HUNGRY FOR THE SUN, IGNORING WHO WILL GRAZE ON THEM – A STEER TODAY, A MASTODON LONG AGO – BUT PERHAPS AWARE OF BEING THE FIRST LINK IN THE FOOD CHAIN. I THINK OF MY EUROPE WHICH HAS NOW BURIED ITS ANCIENT PRAIRIES UNDER A COBWEB OF LETHAL STREETS, RAILWAYS, FIELDS, BUILDINGS AND POISON: ONLY IN THE HUNGARIAN PUSZTA OF THE HORTOBÁGY RESERVE DO

Life on the Prairies
Introduction

HORSE RUN WILD AND FREE AS THEY DID IN THE INFANCY OF HUMANKIND. PRAIRIES HAVE PAID THE PRICE OF THEIR UN-SELFISHNESS TOWARD US! BUT IF ONE HAD THE COURAGE TO VENTURE WHERE HUMANKIND HAS SURRENDERED TO THE HOSTILITY OF THE SURROUNDING LAND, THEN EVERY CONTINENT WILL BE ABLE TO SHOW US THE TRUE MASTER OF THE PRAIRIE: THE MAJESTIC NORTH-AMERICAN BISON, THE PROCESSION OF COYOTES, LYNXES, MINKS AND STUR-DY DUCKS; THE KANGAROOS AND THE ODD MARSUPIAL CREATURES OF THE BARREN EXPANSES OF THE AUSTRALIAN OUTBACK; THE SMALL LEMMINGS OF THE ARCTIC TUNDRA AND, OF COURSE, THE RHEAS OF ARGENTINA.

Europe. This red fox seems to be in a yoga position as it tries to get rid of an annoying parasite.

494 • Asia. Snow isn't a problem for this young Siberian tiger which shows off its muscles as it advances it in leaps and bounds.

495 • Asia. The Siberian tiger, the largest living feline, can weigh more than 660 lbs (300 kg). It hunts by ambushing its prey and making it lose its balance.

496 ● Asia. In a mock fight, these two young Siberian tigers are learning the techniques they'll need for survival once they become adults.

497 ● Asia. Before beginning their solitary adult life, tiger cubs remain with their mothers for two or three years. During this period, they spend their time mainly playing.

498 • North America. The first rays of the sun have surprised this young elk out in the open, but in just a few seconds it will hide in the greenery.

499 • Asia. The Arctic winter forces the reindeer to lengthy migrations in search of food. Reindeer eat lichen, tree bark, pine needles and any blades of grass that survive the icy cold.

500-501 • Asia. Reindeer find their ideal winter pastures on the plains surrounding the Verhojansk Mountains in the Siberian taiga.

502-503 • Asia. The reindeer is the only member of the deer family in which females have antlers as well as males, but males sport antlers in the summer and females in the winter.

504 • Europe. A fox busy hunting in a field in the Camargue.

505 • Europe. The fox will eat most types of food, but is also a good hunter. It prefers birds, mice, rabbits and fowl.

506-507 • Europe. Satiated and satisfied this fox is enjoying a well-deserved afternoon rest on the soft, warm grass, but it always remains on the alert.

508 • Europe. The bean goose of the taiga forms couples which get together every mating season. They recognize each other by their mating dance.

509 • Europe. This great buzzard strutting in an elaborate mating dance in an attempt to win females from its male rivals.

510-511 • Asia. An female Indian rhinoceros with her calf.

512-513 • Oceania. The dingo owes its hunting success mainly to its stamina as a runner. It pursue its prey until it collapses to the ground, exhausted.

514-515 • Oceania. A group of kangaroos drinking on the edge of the Simpson desert, in Australia's Northern Territory.

516-517 • Oceania. More than 50 recognized species of kangaroos exist: all live in Australia, Tasmania and Papua New Guinea.

517 • Oceania. Using their tails as supports, two males challenge each other on the prairie.

Oceania. A family of emu quickly crosses the dry northern Australian prairie in search of food – fruit, seeds, leaves, flowers and grass.

North America. A group of young male elks in the last rays of the autumn sun.

● North America. A majestic male wapiti watches over a group of females in the territory won by defeating rivals.

524-525 • North America. In Yellowstone Park, under the worried gaze of two females, a young elk flounders in a pool of icy water.

526-527 • North America. Hidden by the autumn fog, a small herd of buffalo is drinking from a stream with grassy banks.

528 • North America. Two male caribou confront each other in a duel, crossing their powerful antlers.

528-529 • North America. A defeated caribou retreats, hanging its head in surrender. Fights rarely end in death.

530-531 • South America. A group of female guanaco with their young, which stay close to their mothers for only one year, relaxing in a field of flowers.

532 and 533 • South America. Adult male guanaco are very aggressive with rivals. These young ones are sniffing each other and engaging in mock fights, all part of preparing for adulthood.

534-535 • South America. This guanaco is the lord of its territory, ready to chase away any intruders with ferocious bites.

In the SHADOW of the PEAKS

COLIN MONTEATH

- Europe. Two steenboks confront each other on a snowy slope inside Italy's Gran Paradiso National Park.

In the Shadow of the Peaks

Introduction

Mountain regions of the world – the Himalayas, Andes, Rockies, and the Alps – are among the most powerful and beautiful landscapes on earth. Influenced by the extreme nature of glaciation, high altitude, dry atmosphere and low temperatures, mountain environments have created unique living conditions that make it difficult for the rich diversity of wildlife to scrape out an existence and survive. Mammal and bird species (and also reptiles, insects and plants) have made highly specialized adaptations to enable them to breed, to search

Asia. A Himalayan leopard studies a potential prey.

INTRODUCTION In the Shadow of the Peaks

AND TIEN SHAN MOUNTAINS FOR ITS HIGHLY PRIZED PELT WITH ITS THICK CREAMY GREY FUR WITH BEAUTIFUL BLACK BLOTCHES. THE SNOW LEOPARD IS FOUND FROM THE MOUNTAINS OF MONGOLIA, THROUGH CENTRAL ASIA, THE KARAKORAM AND ACROSS THE HIMALAYAN RANGES FROM LADAKH ON INDIA'S NORTHEAST SHOULDER, TO TIBET, NEPAL AND BHUTAN. HOWEVER, THE SNOW LEOPARD POPULATION IS NOW DRASTICALLY REDUCED BY POACHING, AND IT REMAINS A HIGHLY ELUSIVE CREATURE, RARELY SEEN. EDUCATION AND CONSERVATION EFFORTS REVOLVE AROUND REDUCING THE HUNTING BOTH FOR TROPHIES AND BY FARMERS WHO OFTEN KILL THE CAT AFTER IT HAS TAKEN SOME OF THEIR SHEEP

INTRODUCTION In the Shadow of the Peaks

OR GOATS. THEIR NATURAL PREY IS THE BHARAL (THE HI-
MALAYAN BLUE SHEEP) THAT GRAZES ON THE RANGE'S
HIGH ALPS. I TREASURE THE MEMORY OF FINDING FRESH
SNOW LEOPARD TRACKS IN THE MUD AS MY EXPEDITION
LEFT A REMOTE PART OF THE CHINESE KARAKORAM. I
IMAGINED A GRACEFUL CAT WATCHING US FROM A CLIFF
AS OUR CAMEL CARAVAN HEADED OFF DOWN THE
SHAKSGAM RIVER.

THE FLEET-FOOTED VICUÑA FROM THE PERUVIAN ANDES
ALSO TYPIFIES THE ELEGANCE AND BEAUTY OF A MOUN-
TAIN ANIMAL. SMALLER THAN ITS BETTER KNOWN SOUTH
AMERICAN COUSINS THE LLAMA, ALPACA AND GUANACO
(ALL MEMBERS OF THE CAMELID FAMILY), THE VICUÑA IS

INTRODUCTION In the Shadow of the Peaks

HIGHLY PRIZED FOR ITS VERY FINE, WARM WOOL. VICUÑA ARE STILL FOUND IN THE WILD; HOWEVER, THEY ARE AL-SO FARMED IN PERU FOR THEIR WOOL. THIS IS IN DIRECT CONTRAST TO THE CHIRU (AN ANTELOPE) OF THE TI-BETAN PLATEAU WHEREBY THE ANIMAL IS HUNTED AND KILLED BY POACHERS FOR ITS FINE WOOL CALLED "SHA-TOOSH." SHATOOSH IS TRADED ON THE INTERNATIONAL BLACK MARKET, OFTEN WOVEN INTO DELICATE SHAWLS SO FINE THAT THEY CAN BE PULLED THROUGH A WED-DING RING. POACHERS HAVE PERPETUATED THE MYTH THAT THE ANIMAL'S WOOL IS PLUCKED OR SHORN AND THE ANIMAL IS NOT KILLED.

THE ROCKIES OF NORTH AMERICA NOW HAVE A WELL

INTRODUCTION In the Shadow of the Peaks

DEFINED SERIES OF NATURE RESERVES AND NATIONAL PARKS. AS SUCH, ANIMALS LIKE THE BIG HORN SHEEP AND GRIZZLY BEAR ARE TOTALLY PROTECTED AND THEIR NUMBERS ARE FLOURISHING. WOLVES, HOWEVER, THE NATURAL PREDATOR OF THE BIG HORN SHEEP, ARE STILL TREATED LIKE VERMIN IN MANY PARTS OF USA AND ARE IN NEED OF BETTER PROTECTION TO KEEP A SENSIBLE BALANCE BETWEEN THEM AND SHEEP POPULATIONS.

MOUNTAIN TRAVELERS, BE THEY CLIMBERS, TREKKERS OR SKIERS, ALWAYS CHERISH COMING ACROSS ANIMALS IN THE WILD. THERE IS NOTHING MORE WONDERFUL THAN TO SIT AND OBSERVE THE MOVEMENTS OF ANI-MALS, FOR INSTANCE, A FLOCK OF BHARAL AS THESE

INTRODUCTION In the Shadow of the Peaks

POWERFUL MOUNTAIN SHEEP GRAZE ON THE SIDE OF HIGH RIDGELINE. IN COUNTRIES LIKE BHUTAN, WHERE ALL WILDLIFE IS TOTALLY PROTECTED, BHARAL DO NOT FEAR HUMANS AS A PREDATOR. IT IS SURPRISING HOW CLOSE ONE CAN GET TO BHARAL BY WALKING SLOWLY AND QUIETLY.

MOUNTAIN ENVIRONMENTS ALL OVER THE WORLD NEED BETTER MANAGEMENT SO THAT THEIR WILDLIFE IS PRO-TECTED FROM LOSS OF HABITAT OR THE PRESSURE OF BEING HUNTED. CONSERVATION AND EDUCATION PRO-GRAMS NEED MORE SUPPORT SO: THERE NEEDS TO BE GROWING AWARENESS, PARTICULARLY AMONG LOCAL FARMERS OR HUNTERS, THAT MOUNTAIN WILDLIFE IS

In the Shadow of the Peaks

Introduction

WORTH FAR MORE ALIVE THAN DEAD. IT HAS BEEN CLEARLY DEMONSTRATED THAT THERE IS MORE PROFIT IS PRESERVING WHALES FOR THE WHALE-WATCHING TOURISM INDUSTRY THAN THERE IS IN ALLOWING THEIR SLAUGHTER BY WHALERS, WHO SELL WHALE MEAT IN JAPAN. LIKEWISE IT SHOULD BE DEMONSTRATED THAT HIGH-MOUNTAIN SPECIES ARE WORTH SAVING AND THAT WELL MANAGED, CONSERVATION-ORIENTED MOUNTAIN TRAVEL AND GUIDED PHOTOGRAPHIC TOURS ARE MORE PROFITABLE TO THE HOST NATIONS THAN AN ILLEGAL TRADE IN ANIMAL SKINS.

- South America. The male Andean condor has a fleshy crest about 4 inches (10 cm) long on its bald head.

Europe. December is a very important month for male steenboks; it's when they engage in violent duels to win a mate.

Europe. Stags in the Bialowieza Forest in Poland are a protected species.

552 ● Europe. Because of its great talent of adaptation, foxes are widespread in many European countries. They usually live in well-hidden dens in the forest and use them as bases for hunting. Foxes are very agile animals, seldom hindered by obstacles.

553 ● Asia. A golden eagle flying above the snows of the Golden Mountains, in Russia's Altai region.

554 • Europe. A mountain hare balancing itself to reach some berries.

555 • Europe. A red squirrel protecting its meager food reserve between its paws.

556 • Europe. A marmot cub learning how to socialize from its mother. Here, it's "tuning" its sense of smell in a very important "training" session.

557 • Europe. An ermine in winter is perfectly camouflaged in the snow but it's still always vigilant because camouflage alone can't guarantee safety.

558 • Africa. Abyssinian wolves, considered to be the world's rarest Canidae, live in packs.

559 • Africa. Abyssinian wolves survive only on seven Ethiopian high plateaus, at altitudes of between 9500 and 13,150 ft (3000 and 4000 m).

• Africa. Gelada baboons, native to Ethiopia, live in groups comprised of hundreds of members. They communicate with each other using loud, shrill cries. They live at a high altitude with little vegetation, and, unlike other baboons, spend more time on the ground than in tree-tops.

● Asia. Japanese macaques bathing in warm, thermal waters in the Jigokudani National Park. These animals are excellent swimmers and, in the winter, they often seek warmth in the waters of this hot pool.

564 • Asia. Two Japanese macaques grooming; this activity has fundamental social importance.

564-565 • Asia. A female Japanese macaque is carrying her baby on her back.

566 ● Asia. Thick fur keeps snow leopards warm. Here one is leaping about in the Nanda Devi National Park in India.

567 ● Asia. A snow leopard in the Altai mountains, Russia, looks around suspiciously.

568 • Asia. This magnificent snow leopards is seen in the photo as it attacks its prey.

569 • Asia. Two young snow leopards resting, probably after a hunt, using the snow as their pillow.

North America. A Dall goat resting in a meadow in the Denali National Park mountains, Alaska.

572 and 573 • Europe. The golden eagle has a hooked beak which it uses to tear its prey apart.

574-575 • North America. Two Rocky Mountain rams prepare for battle.

576 ● North America. A mountain goat teaches its kids to negotiate the crags in the Fjords National Park, Kenai, Alaska.

577 ● North America. Mountain goats are expert climbers. Their most obvious features are their short legs and their well-developed shoulder muscles.

578 and *579* • South America. Guanacos are herbivores used to living in harsh environments at high altitudes. They eat any type of vegetation and can go without drinking for a long time.

580-581 • South America. A herd of alpacas is migrating to an Andean high plateau in search of food.

The CALL of the FOREST

FRANCESCO PETRETTI

- Eurasia. The wolf is the protagonist of woodland life in forests in North America, Europe and Asia.

The Call of the Forest

Introduction

Throughout the hot summer months, leaving sunny meadows and entering woods of beech-trees reminds us of the cool relief that places of worship, massive and impressive, bring about . . . peace of mind. Or, in other words, when we walk within dense woods smelling of mold, the sight of cool calm water running in the soft soil, the towering trees reaching for the sun while intertwined with thick, often sweet smelling vines, and the presence of trunks and branches fallen to the ground, slowly rotting, feeding the mushrooms and thus renewing life –

• Asia. Broad-leaved forests with a thick bamboo underbrush are the habitat of the giant panda.

INTRODUCTION The Call of the Forest

ALL THESE COMBINE TO OFFER US A MYSTICAL EXPERIENCE. WHEN MEANDERING THROUGH THESE WOODS ONE HEARS THE HOARSE BARK OF ROE-DEER, THE COOING OF WOODPIGEONS, THE WARBLING OF MISTLE THRUSHES, THE DRUMMING OF GREEN WOODPECKERS ON BRANCHES AND DRY TRUNKS ALMOST AS IF DELIBERATELY CHOSEN TO AMPLIFY THEIR BEAT. SIMULTANEOUSLY, ANCIENT WOODS WITH BEECH-TREES, YEWS AND HOLLIES ARE COMMONLY THE HABITAT OF ONE OF THE SNEAKIEST ANIMALS WITHIN THE EUROPEAN FAUNA, THE WILDCAT. THEY ARE HUNTERS, PREDATORY, HARD TO SPOT AND DANGEROUS. THE TRACES OF THEIR PRESENCE IN OUR FORESTS ARE IRREFUTABLE.

INTRODUCTION The Call of the Forest

IN THE AUTUMN (SEPTEMBER/OCTOBER) MOST MOUNTAIN RANGES QUICKLY GIVE WAY TO A VAST ARRAY OF COLORS. FOR A FEW WEEKS THEY SEEM AS IF IN FLAMES: MAPLE TREE LEAVES TURN FROM GREEN TO RED AND ORANGE, MANNA TREES FROM YELLOW TO PURPLE, BEECH TREES FROM YELLOW TO PLUM AND LATER ON FADE OUT TO A RUST OUTBURST. THE SHRUBS ARE NO LESS IMPRESSIVE: CORNEL TREES TURN BLOOD RED, PRICK WOODS YELLOW/BROWN, EVEN THE HUMBLE BLACKBERRIES MANAGE TO DISPLAY RED AND YELLOW SPOTS. EVERY TREE AND BUSH ENGAGES ANNUALLY IN THIS "SHOW-OFF" COMPETITION! THE SHOW DOES NOT LAST LONG: TREE LEAVES GATHER AT THEIR FEET AND

The Call of the Forest

Introduction

BRANCHES GROW BARE. WINTER IS ON ITS WAY. IT IS ALL FOR THE BEST; WITHIN THE GROUND NEW LIFE IS COMING INTO BEING. BEECH TREE SEEDS, OAK ACORNS, MAPLE SAMARAS ALL ARE BRINGING ABOUT THE BIRTH OF YOUNG TREES READY TO WAKE UP AND JOIN US. WITHIN A RELATIVELY SHORT TIME, THIN BUT STRONG ROOTS, AIDED BY BACTERIA AND MULTIPLE TINY ANIMALS WILL CONTRIBUTE TO THE GERMINATION OF YOUNG TREES WHICH IN TURN WILL GIVE RISE TO HEALTHY NEW FORESTS. THE PREORDAINED CYCLE OF LIFE REPEATS ONCE AGAIN.

589 ● Europe. The sea eagle usually builds its nest on the cliffs along the coast, but in Eastern Europe it builds them on the tallest trees of the forest.

590-591 ● Eurasia. A young male deer is leading its harem of females. This species originates from the Middle East.

592 • Europe. The deer selects its grasses and plants with care. Its favorite plant is dandelion.

593 • Europe. Deer vocalize by grunting or bleating. They also communicate through their very refined sense of smell.

594 and 595 • Europe. Even though foxes can live in a wide variety of habitats, they seek the shelter of the forest to raise their cubs (right).

596-597 • Europe. A fox hunting for insects and other small prey in a clearing in the forest.

● Europe. The lynx is
the rarest of all the
large predators in the
European forests but its
numbers are increasing
in many regions of
the Alps.

● Europe. Like all felines, the female lynx takes good care of her young and she takes her cubs to a new den if she senses any danger.

Europe. Two lynxes
courting in a rather
aggressive way during the
mating season.

Europe. A golden eagle has captured an unlucky prey which had entrusted its safety to its mimetic white color. Eagles are not a migratory species and will spend their winters even in the high mountains and northernmost areas of their territory.

● Europe. The brown bear and the polar bear are the two largest land carnivores, but neither attacks man. The largest of these bears can exceed 10 ft (3 m) in height when they stand on their hind legs.

608-609 ● Europe. It is difficult for the large brown bear to live in trees.

609 ● America. The baribal, or American black bear, however, is more agile in trees.

Europe. Male brown bears, which don't hibernate in the winter, incessantly hunt for food in the snow.

612 • Europe. The red squirrel, nicknamed "the forest elf," is a natural acrobat and shows off its skills in the Eurasian pine forests.

613 • Europe. Young squirrels gradually learn their parents' tree climbing skills.

● Europe. Not much bigger than a sparrow, the pygmy owl is the smallest European nocturnal predatory bird. It builds its nests in tree trunks hollowed out by woodpeckers.

Europe. Young tawny owls of the Urals on a tree branch, waiting for their parents to bring them food. These birds leave the nest when very young, before they have fully grown their feathers.

618-619 • Europe. The tawny owl of Lapland lives in a broad area of the taiga throughout the northern world.

619 • Europe. The tawny owl doesn't build its own nests but uses those built by other animals, some of which are not birds.

620-621 • Europe. A sea eagle with an adult deer: it couldn't have killed such a big prey so the deer must have been killed by other predators or died because of bad weather.

622 ● Europe. A goshawk confronts the
snowfall with the calm of a predator
confident in its excellent skills.

622-623 ● Europe. The peregrine
doesn't mind the rain. It's one of the most
vigorous of the predatory birds.

624 • America. At dawn, on the edge of a forest, four young Virginia deer are surprised by
the photographer's click.

625 • America. A mule deer feeding one of its fawns while the other one waits its turn.
Females stay in the thickest part of the forest to protect their fawns.

626 • America. The puma is one of the most widespread predators; it is found throughout the American continents from Alaska to Tierra del Fuego.

627 • America. Puma cubs have black spots. Their mother takes good cares of them and carries them gently by the scruff of the neck.

628-629 and *630-631* • America. Life is even more difficult in the forest after a snowfall because the animals must come out into the open where predators can easily spot them.

America. The wolf's life is greatly influenced by the movements of the prey it hunts. In North America, it follows caribou and elk, while in Europe, it tracks deer and boars.

America. Left – A wolf cub learning to howl. Howling is important because it keeps the pack together. Right – A female carrying her cub to a safer den. In wolf packs, only the dominant pair reproduces.

638 and 638-639 ● America. The
red lynx hides its cubs to protect
them; they are in danger even from
male lynxes.

640-641 ● America. A family of
foxes is following a very smelly
skunk but doesn't dare to get too
close to it.

America. A black bear is crossing a rocky canyon in the same way a man would. These animals are very intelligent. Some experts believe they are as intelligent as apes.

America. No animal can win against an adult brown bear. These bears will defend their food even from a wolf pack.

646 ● America. A black bear, also called a baribal, easily climbs trees.

647 ● America. These black bear cubs are climbing a tree to escape from their worst enemy: the brown bear or "grizzly".

648, 649 and 650-651 • The brown bear is a solitary animal though it spends much time with its mother and siblings when it is young. Bear cubs learn their survival and hunting skills by playing with their siblings and by imitating the behavior of their mother. In America, the brown bear which is also found in Europe and Asia, is called the grizzly bear.

Between LAND and WATER

CRISTINA PERABONI

America. The unmistakable heron, in the first rays of the morning sun.
The heron is always found near fresh water.

INTRODUCTION Between Land and Water

...Rank reeds and lush, slimy water-plants sent an odour of decay and a heavy miasmatic vapour onto our faces, while a false step plunged us more than once thigh-deep into the dark, quivering mire...

So wrote Sir Arthur Conan Doyle, in his novel *The Hound of the Baskervilles*, describing the gloomy environment, the wet and thick atmosphere of the peat bog where horrible crimes are committed.

It's true, marshes, bogs, pools, lagoons are words that evoke strong feelings and recall dark and remote, dangerous, forbidden places. Nonetheless the water is in itself the symbol of life, and life is unrelenting where water abounds. During

INTRODUCTION Between Land and Water

SPRING AND SUMMER, UNDERNEATH THE EXPANSE OF WATER LILIES, IN THE THICK REEDS, AMONG THE TANGLE OF THE MANGROVES, THE EXTRAORDINARY SHOW OF NATURE'S VITALITY TAKES PLACE UNABATED – BUT MOSTLY HIDDEN TO OUR DISTRUSTFUL EYES. ON THE OTHER HAND, THE HERON KNOWS HE WILL BE ABLE TO CHOSE HIS DINNER AMONG HUNDREDS OF DIFFERENT SMALL ANIMALS WHO TEEM BETWEEN HIS LONG LEGS WHEN HE STRUTS ACROSS THE MUDDY WATER. JUST LIKE HIM, MIGRATORY BIRDS COME SWARMING, AND FEASTING LAVISHLY AT THIS SUMPTUOUS TABLE. THE SUMMER MARSH IS THE WORLD OF THE AMPHIBIANS: THE MIRACLE OF METAMORPHOSIS REOCCURS CYCLICALLY, THE TADPOLE TURNS INTO A FROG AND SHE, ALONG WITH THOUSANDS OF HER SISTERS,

Between Land and Water

Introduction

FILLS THE NIGHT WITH A CONCERT OF DEAFENING CROAK-ING. FIERCE ARMIES OF MOSQUITOES, HATED BY HUMANS, PROVIDE AN INEXTINGUISHABLE RESOURCE FOR THE ANI-MALS GREEDY FOR INSECTS, THUS COMPLETING THE CIR-CLE. THE EFFORTLESS FLIGHT OF THE DRAGONFLIES GIVES THESE GLOOMY PLACES A TOUCH OF GRACE, OF WHICH MANY CANNOT SEE THE CHARM. BUT DAYS ARE DRAWING IN; THE AIR GETS COLDER, THE MIGRANTS LEAVE ONCE AGAIN AND ACROSS THE WETLANDS SILENCE SUBSIDES. FOR MONTHS EVERYTHING WILL SEEM DEAD, EXCEPT THAT GROWTH WILL START ANEW IN THE SPRING SPRING, WHEN WILDLIFE WILL BLOSSOM ONCE MORE.

• America. This butterfly has chosen a strange landing spot but the jacar, or black crocodile, of the Brazilian swamps is waiting for bigger prey.

658 • Europe. Lovingly protected by its mother's wings, this flamingo chick is peeking out from the feathers of its comfortable nest.

659 • Europe. This chick's beak is very different from the characteristic one of its mother, on which it totally depends for food.

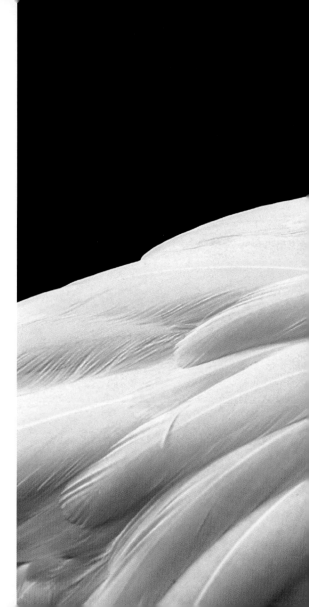

America. The flamingo's beak enables it to filter the small shrimp it eats but also obliges it to take a strange position. Flamingos owe their splendid coloring to carotene found in their food.

Europe. Its large size and proud appearance make the marine eagle unmistakable. It is found in coastal marshes where it hunts large fish. Young eagles, which have spotted feathers, are most often found in groups in the areas rich in fish.

664 and 645 • Europe. The elegance of the swan's flight has inspired legends, artists, musicians and poets. The royal swan (right) is the most beautiful of all. It parades in a magnificent way to scare off rivals and when it courts a mate.

666-667 • Europe. Sometimes, graceful swans are also seen in clownish positions which are truly funny, even though stemming from aggressive intentions.

668 • Europe. The wild goose is powerful and untiring and can fly for thousands of miles.

669 • Africa. The South African shelduck is able to survive on the scarce water found in deserts like that of Namibia.

670-671 • Europe. A mother duck swims with her ducklings, somewhat protected by her mimetic plumage.

672 ● Europe. Herons are expert fishers. Sometimes, they catch fish which seem to be too large but the heron swallows them head first with ease.

673 ● Europe. This ash heron is moving slowly in the marshy waters ready to capture fish which come close to it, mistaking its long legs for reeds.

Asia and Europe. Boars coming from two places very far from each other – Rajasthan and the Camargue – show the same impetus as they race through the marshland. The boar is the ancestor of the domestic pig and consist of only one species with numerous sub-species. Its weight ranges from 265 lbs (120 kg) to three times that mass.

Europe. This osprey is sharp sighted like all predator birds. It has captured its prey; this sometimes weighs more than it does. This bird has a wing span of 70 inches (180 cm) and weighs only about 3.3 lbs (1.5 kg)!

America. The greater blue heron nests in the wetlands of Northern and Central America. It makes its large nest of leaves and twigs in forked tree branches, even at 165 ft (50 m) above ground.

● Europe. A large carp can provide ash heron nestlings with a good meal. On the right, this heron ambushes a carp unsuspectingly swimming beneath its beak in the shallow water.

682 • America. During its mating season, the greater white heron has beautiful feathers which are longer and thinner than usual and which are very ornamental.

683 • America. Though for many decades hunted for its beautiful plumage, the graceful American greater white heron can be often seen in the Florida Everglades.

684 ● Europe. A kingfisher feeding a chick. These birds kill their prey before eating it by beating its head against a tree branch or against a rock.

685 ● Europe. This kingfisher is coming out of the water without having captured a fish. Sometimes, its dives aren't successful.

686 and 686-687 ● Africa. Carrion is an easy meal so even a great predator like the fishing eagle is willing to fight off the weaker beaks of the marabs for a piece of flamingo.

688-689 ● Africa. These lechwe antelopes (which have many females without horns) have been frightened by potential danger and are racing away across the swamp.

690 • Africa. Waiting for the rainy season, these elephants cool off during the hottest time of the day near this pool, one of the last to survive the dry season.

691 • Africa. Surrounded by cattle herons, mamma elephant patiently awaits her youngster before joining the rest of the herd.

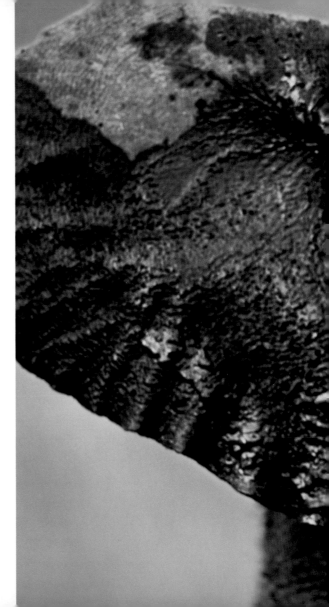

Africa. This young elephant is taking a savannah mud bath to keep its skin from cracking and to rid itself of insects.

● Africa. To demonstrate their dominance, male buffaloes take charge of the pool where they take mud baths to protect themselves from the heat and from bugs.

696 • Africa. The skin of the hippopotamus is very sensitive to the sun; thus it is obliged to spend the greatest part of the day submerged in water.

697 • Africa. The wide open mouth of the hippopotamus boasts enormous tusk-like teeth which keep enemies away. This ferocious looking animal is actually a herbivore.

● Africa. This
hippopotamus is very
still and almost
completely submerged
in the water. Just its
nostrils emerge so that
it can breathe during
its "siesta".

700 ● Africa. The small sitalunga antelope lives in the marshy areas of Africa. This one looks very funny as it scratches its ear.

701 ● Africa. This young baboon is playing in the water like a child.

702 and 702-703 ● Africa. White pelicans (left) eating in the shallow water. During mating season, the feathers of the males (right) take on a pink coloring which the females find attractive.

704-705 ● Africa. The lesser flamingo is recognized by its entirely black beak.

706 ● Asia. The Indian Barasingha stag prefers wetlands. This sensitive animal is hunted by many predators.

706-707 ● Asia. The sambar stag, here seen in the company of two crows, is rarely seen far from water.

Asia. An orangutan drinking from a stream. For centuries, man has hunted this animal; in its eyes we see fear but also tenderness.

Asia. The crab-eating macaco is a good swimmer. This animal mainly eats vegetables, with the addition of small amounts of eggs and meats.

● Asia. This frightening lizard lives in
the swamps of Southeast Asia (left).
It reaches a length of 4.2 ft (1.3 m).
The reticulated python (right) is the
longest, though not the largest,
snake in the world.

714 and 715 • America. The giant otter is at perfect ease among the water lilies in the open waters of the Pantanal. The otter is an excellent predator and has few natural enemies.

716-717 • America. Only the eyes of these two leopard frogs emerge from the water, the best way to see a heron before being seen.

718 ● America. With its neck bent, this blue heron is ready to ambush prey from its hiding place in the aquatic vegetation of the Florida Everglades.

719 ● America. The slow-moving, shallow river in the Florida Everglades is a paradise for the blue heron which feeds solely on fish and frogs.

720 and 720-721 • America. This alligator looks like a fallen tree trunk, which makes it easy for him to find unsuspecting prey.

722-723 • Africa. Nile crocodiles are expert swimmers.

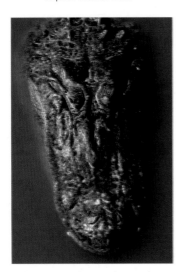

724-725 • America. Flamingos group together in the Galapagos lagoons where they know they will find abundant food.

726-727 • America. The Everglades are the last refuge of the Florida puma.

AUTHORS Biographies

VALERIA MANFERTO DE FABIANIS

She is the editor of the series. Valeria Manferto De Fabianis was born in Vercelli, Italy and studied arts at the Università Cattolica del Sacro Cuore in Milan, graduating with a degree in philosophy.

She is an enthusiastic traveler and nature lover. She has collaborated on the production of television documentaries and articles for the most prestigious Italian specialty magazines and has also written many photography books.

She co-founded Edizioni White Star in 1984 with Marcello Bertinetti and is the editor-in-chief.

CRISTINA MARIA BANFI,

who was born in 1966, has a degree in Natural Sciences. Her work is aimed at popularizing science, with young people as a primary target. Banfi is vice-president of the Museum Education Association and since 1994 has headed the educational services of Milan's Municipal Museum of Natural History. She organizes cultural events, plans educational courses and encounters in the sphere of environmental education and natural sciences.

GIORGIO G. BARDELLI,

who was born in Milan in 1965, has a degree in Natural Sciences. He is curator of the scientific collections of the Vertebrate Zoology Section of the Municipal Museum of Natural History, Milan and is also engaged in educational activities aimed at the public and schools. He has published scientific, museological and popular works.

ANGELA SERENA ILDOS,

was born in 1967 and graduated in Natural Sciences. Currently she works in a number of scientific fields; she is manager of the educational section of Milan's Natural History Civic Museum and is a lecturer in a number of cultural institutes, including the Università Popolare and the Libera Università Lombarda. She has published various books on nature and animals, and for Edizioni White Star she wrote and edited *The Great National Parks of the World*.

COLIN MONTEATH,

who was born in New Zealand, is a polar and mountain photographer

who has had spent 28 years working in Antarctica and three in the Arctic. He has also been involved in expeditions and magazine assignments in many parts of the Himalayas. Monteath has worked in Antarctica for the New Zealand government as a field operations officer and as a freelance wildlife and mountaineering guide. He also runs Hedgehog House Photographic library, which specializes in natural history, the environment and the world's polar and mountain regions.

CRISTINA PERABONI, who was born in 1956 in Milan, has a degree in Veterinary Medicine and decided to dedicate her efforts to teaching and popularizing science at the Municipal Museum of Natural History in Milan, where she is one of the managers of the Education Section, which the Museum Education Association has run since 1994. She also works for several publishers, chiefly editing works for young people.

FRANCESCO PETRETTI, graduated in Biological Sciences, with a specialization in Zoology. Since 1983 he has been working in the environmental sector and is a member of the Scientific Committee of the World Wildlife Fund (Italy) and the Species Survival Commission of the World Conservation Union (IUCN). Since 1990 he has been active in communicating and popularizing of environmental themes through television, radio and publishing.

ALBERTO LUCA RECCHI is a journalist, documentary maker and photographer. The giants of the sea are his passion, and in order to encounter them in their native environments he has participated in expeditions all over the world. Recchi has written numerous books on the sea, including many with Piero and Alberto Angela. He was also creator of the Shark Exhibition, which was a huge success at Palazzo delle Esposizioni in Rome and at the Arengario Museum in Milan.

RITA MABEL SCHIAVO, a biologist and naturalist, with a special passion for ethology, has chosen to dedicate her efforts to popularizing these interests, drawing on her skills to illustrate and explain the marvelous world that surrounds us. She is a founding member of the Museum Education Association and one of the managers of the Museums and Territory educational services of Milan's Municipal Museum of Natural History.

INDEX

A

Abyssinian wolf, 558c
Adelie penguin, 280c,
    288c, 292c
Africa, 14c, 40c, 43,
    46c, 48c, 53c, 55c,
    59c, 60c, 66c, 70c,
    72c, 74c, 80c, 82c,
    84c, 87c, 88c, 90c,
    94c, 100c, 103c,
    105c, 107c, 108c,
    111c, 113c, 115c, 117c,
    118c, 120c, 122c,
    124c, 127c, 128c,
    130c, 134c, 136,
    138, 145c, 146c,
    148c, 151c, 152c,
    157c, 159c, 160c,
    162c, 164c, 166c,
    169c, 170c, 180c,
    206c, 212c, 222c,
    296c, 300c, 302c,
    304c, 309c, 311c,
    312c, 314c, 318c,
    321c, 322c, 324c,
    327c, 328c, 333c,
    558c, 560c, 562c,
    564c, 668c, 686c,
    690c, 692c, 695c,
    696c, 699c, 700c,
    702c, 714c, 720c
Alaska, 14c, 30c, 231,
    239c, 258c, 626c
Albatross, 14c, 268c,
    364c
Albino dromedary,
    304c
Alligator, 14c
Allobates frog, 14c
Alpaca, 542, 578c
Altai Mountains
    (Russia), 552c
Amazon rain forest,
    16
America, 197c, 624c,

626c, 629c, 632c,
    634c, 636c, 638c,
    643c, 645c, 646c,
    648c, 652c, 656c,
    660c, 678c, 682c,
    714c, 718c, 720c
American pelican,
    366c
Andes condor, 546c
Andes, 342c
Anemone, 360c, 464c
Antarctic polar circle,
    280c
Antarctica, 14c, 228,
    231, 232, 235, 236c,
    272c, 278c, 280c,
    283c, 286c, 288c,
    291c, 292c
Antelope, 53c, 55c,
    118c, 140, 328c,
    700c
Ara parrot, 214c, 220c
Arctic fox, 254c
Arctic Ocean, 228
Arctic Sea, 228
Arctic, 228, 231
Argentina, 200c
Asia, 136, 136c, 174c,
    176c, 178c, 184c,
    186c, 188c, 190c,
    192c, 194c, 206c,
    218c, 494c, 496c,
    498c, 508c, 538c,
    552c, 566c, 568c,
    582c, 584c, 648c,
    674c, 706c, 709c,
    711c, 712c
Atlantic Ocean, 14c,
    276c, 364c, 366c,
    371c, 372c, 376c,
    381c, 382c, 384c,
    389c, 392c, 406c,
    410c, 414c, 416c,
    422c, 424c, 430c,
    432c, 441c, 472c

Australia, 234, 272c,
    344c, 517c
Australian pelican, 366c

B

Baboon, 44, 118c,
    120c, 166c, 700c
Bald eagle, 371c
Baral (blue sheep), 542
Barracuda, 356, 441c,
    444c
Bean goose, 508c
Beluga (white dolphin),
    266c
Bering Sea, 258c
Bhutan, 545
Black bear (baribal),
    609c, 646c
Black cayman (jacaré),
    656c
Black right whale, 406c
Boar, 632c, 674c
Borneo, 194c
Bottlenose dolphin,
    376c
Brown bear (grizzly),
    606c, 609c, 610c,
    646c, 648c
Brown pelican, 414c,
    416c
Bryde's whale, 408c
Buffalo, 55c, 80c, 695c
Butterfly fish, 471c,
    472c

C

California, 429c, 426c
Camargue, 504c, 674c
Cape fox, 302c
Caracal (African lynx),
    157c, 311c
Carangid, 444c
Caribou, 231, 528c,
    632c
Carp, 681c

Cheetah, 14c, 60c,
    66c, 70c, 72c, 74c
Chimpanzee, 159c,
    160c, 162c, 164c
Clownfish, 360c, 464c
Common dolphin,
    375c, 381c
Congo Plain, 148c
Copper shark, 392c
Cortez Sea, 429c
Crested penguin, 272c
Crocodile, 103c

D

Dall's goat, 571c
Deer, 592c, 619c
Denali Park (Alaska),
    571c
Dendrobates frog, 142c
Dingo, 508c
Diurnal octopus, 456c
Douc langur, 184c
Duck hawk, 622c
Duck, 668c

E

Elephant, 45, 46, 74c,
    80c, 82c, 84c, 88c,
    169c, 690c
Elk, 30c, 488c, 498c,
    632c
Emperor penguin, 14c,
    233, 234, 280c,
    284c, 291c, 292c
Emu, 347c, 519c
Ermine, 556c
Europe, 492c, 504c,
    508c, 536c, 549c,
    550c, 552c, 554c,
    556c, 572c, 582c,
    588c, 592c, 594c,
    599c, 600c, 602c,
    604c, 606c, 609c,
    610c, 612c, 614c,
    616c, 619c, 622c,

632c, 648c, 658c, 663c, 664c, 668c, 672c, 674c, 676c, 681c, 684c
Everglades (Florida), 14c, 682c, 718c, 720c

F

Falkland Islands, 14c, 268c, 276c
Fallow deer, 588c
Far East, 186c
Fawn, 624c
Fennec, 304c
Fish eagle, 686c
Flamingo, 658c, 660c, 686c, 720c
Florida, 14c
Four-leaf jellyfish, 436c
Fox, 504c, 552c, 594c, 638c
French Guiana, 14c
Frog, 208c

G

Galapagos Islands, 426c, 478c, 480c, 482c, 720c
Gazelle, 30c, 108c, 111c
Gecko, 222c
Gelada baboon, 560c
Gemsbok antelope, 14c
Gemsbok, 314c, 318c
Gerenuk, 108c
Giraffe, 90c, 94c, 122c
Glass frog, 212c
Gnu, 16, 94c, 100c, 103c
Golden eagle, 552c, 572c, 604c

Goliath grouper, 458c
Gorilla, 14c, 134c, 145c, 146c
Goshawk, 622c
Gran Paradiso Park, 536c
Gray heron, 672c
Gray seal, 420c
Great blue egret, 678c
Great white egret, 682c
Great white shark, 26c, 352c, 357, 358, 384c
Green turtle, 436c, 439c, 444c
Greenland seal, 260c, 262c, 264c
Guanaco, 542, 578c

H

Halcyon, 231
Hammer-fish, 394c
Harenna forest, 140
Harris buzzard, 340c
Hawksbill turtle, 439c
Heron, 652c, 672c
Herring gull, 368c
Himalayan leopard, 538c
Hippopotamus, 696c, 699c
Horned viper, 300c
Hummingbird, 180c
Humpback whale, 354c, 396c, 398c, 400c, 402c, 404c
Hyena, 72c, 117c
Hymenoptera, 180c

I

Ibex, 536c, 549c
Impala, 107c, 111c, 170c
India, 136c

Indian Barasingha deer, 706c
Indian Ocean, 142, 352c, 360c, 375c, 387c, 392c, 408c, 436c, 444c, 464c, 467c, 471c, 472c, 477c
Indian rhinoceros, 508c
Indochina, 136c
Indonesia, 136c

J

Jaguar, 200c, 205c
Japanese macaco, 560c, 564c
Jigokudani Park, 562c

K

Kangaroo, 344c
Karakorum, 541, 542
Kenai Fjords Park (Alaska), 576c
Kenya, 14c, 30c
Killer whale, 268c, 432c, 434c
Kingfisher, 684c
Kittiwake, 231
Koala, 198c
Kudu, 53c

L

La Madeleine Island, 262c, 264c
Lama, 542
Lapland owl, 619c
Lechwe antelope, 686c
Leopard (serval), 157c
Leopard frog, 714c
Leopard seal, 286c, 288c
Leopard, 30c, 40c, 124c, 128c, 130c, 206c, 542

Liana snake, 222c
Lion fish, 468c
Lion, 44, 48c, 59c, 60c, 72c
Lynx, 599c, 600c, 602c, 638c

M

Macaco, 711c
Madagascar, 152c, 170c
Mandrill, 166c
Manta ray, 452c, 455c
Marmot, 556c
Mediterranean Sea, 368c
Meerkat, 322c, 324c
Mexico, 200c
Middle East, 588c
Minor flamingo, 702c
Moloch, 350c
Moth, 214c
Mountain goat, 576c
Mountain hare, 554c
Munk's manta ray, 451c
Musk-ox, 231

N

Namibia desert, 296c, 321c
Namibia, 14c, 16, 668c
Nanda Devi Park (India), 566c
New Guinea, 517c
New Zealand, 234, 272c, 422c, 426c
Nile crocodile, 720c
Nile, 100c, 139
North America, 14c, 30c, 226c, 239c, 240c, 244c, 246c, 248c, 254c, 256c, 258c, 260c, 262c,

264c, 266c, 268c, 335c, 336c, 338c, 340c, 488c, 498c, 521c, 522c, 525c, 528c, 571c, 572c, 576c, 582c, 632c, 648c
North Pole, 268c
North Sea, 419c, 420c
Norway, 419c

O

Oceania, 26c, 198c, 228c, 272c, 276c, 284c, 344c, 347c, 348c, 350c, 508c, 517c, 519c
Ocelot, 208c
Octopus, 376c
Orango, 30c, 186c, 188c, 190c, 192c
Orangutan, 709c
Osprey, 676c
Ostrich, 321c, 322c
Otarda, 508c
Otter, 714c
Owl, 340c

P

Pacific Ocean, 26c, 354c, 360c, 366c, 391c, 394c, 396c, 398c, 400c, 402c, 404c, 408c, 412c, 420c, 422c, 424c, 426c, 434c, 436c, 439c, 448c, 451c, 452c, 455c, 456c, 458c, 468c, 472c, 478c, 480c, 482c, 484c
Panther, 206c
Papua penguin, 278c
Patched jackal, 122c,

309c
Penguin, 233
Phyllomedusa frog, 182c
Polar bear, 14c, 226c, 231, 239c, 240c, 244c, 246c, 248c, 606c
Proboscis monkey, 194c
Puffer, 480c
Puffin, 231, 419c
Puma, 335c, 336c, 338c, 626c
Pygmy owl, 614c

Q

Queensland gecko, 348c

R

Rajasthan, 674c
Ram (wether), 572c
Red deer, 592c, 632c
Red fox, 492c
Red Sea, 376c, 444c
Red squirrel, 554c, 612c
Rhinopias aphanes, 467c
Rocky Mountains, 572c
Royal penguin, 228c
Russia, 14c
Rwanda, 14c

S

Sahara desert, 157c, 298
Sambar deer, 706c
Sand cat, 312c
Sanetti high plateau, 140
Sardine, 356, 387c, 392c
Satiride butterfly, 214c

Savannah, 16, 43, 44, 46, 55c, 74c, 105c, 124c
Screaming gecko, 333c
Sea eagle, 588c, 619c, 663c
Sea elephant, 424c
Sea lion, 426c, 429c, 430c, 480c, 482c
Seal, 228, 230, 233, 234
Seal, 30c
Serpent, 115c
Serval, 115c
Shagskam River, 542
Siberian tiger, 14c, 494c, 496c
Simpson desert, 508c
Sitatunga, 700c
Skunk, 638c
Sloth, 200c
Snow leopard, 566c, 568c
Sole, 356
South Africa, 234
South African ruddy shelduck, 668c
South America, 30c, 142c, 180c, 182c, 200c, 205c, 208c, 214c, 220c, 276c, 278c, 342c, 532c, 546c, 578c
South Seas, 232
Spencer's frog, 348c
Sperm whale, 14c, 356, 408c, 410c
Spotted dolphin, 372c, 376c
Steller's sea lion, 480c
Sumatra, 30c, 174c
Swan, 664c

T

Tamarin, 197c
Tasmania, 272c, 517c
Tibet, 541
Tien shan, 541
Tierra del Fuego, 626c
Tiger shark, 389c
Tiger, 136c, 174c, 176c, 178c
Tuna, 356

U

Ural owl, 616c

V

Verhojansk Mountains, 498c
Verreaux langur, 170c
Viper, 152c, 222c, 314c
Virginia deer, 624c

W

Walrus, 230, 231, 256c, 258c
Weddell's seal, 236c
Whale-shark, 412c
White bear, 244c
White fox, 231
White pelican, 429c, 702c
White rhinoceros, 113c
Wild goose, 668c
Wolf, 30c, 632c, 634c, 636c, 645c
Wrangel's Island, 230

Y

Yellow monitor, 218c, 712c
Yellow moray eel, 468c
Yellowstone Park, 525c

Z

Zebra, 45, 66c, 94c, 105c

PHOTO CREDITS

PHOTO CREDITS

Robert C. Nunnington/Getty Images: pages 24-25
Rolf Nussbaumer/Naturepl.com/ Contrasto: pages 366, 716-717
R. Oggioni/PandaPhoto: pages 608-609
Olycom: page 181
Michael Patrick O'Neill/NHPA/Photoshot: page 468
Pete Oxford/Naturepl.com/Contrasto: pages 196-197, 210-211, 212-213, 216-217, 222, 486-487, 724-725
Oxford Scientific Films/Auscape: pages 326-327, 327, 528, 577
PandaPhoto: page 209
Papilio/Alamy: pages 528-529
D. Parer & E. Parer-Cook/HedgeHogHouse: page 423
Andrew Parkinson/Naturepl.com/ Contrasto: page 420
David Paynter/Agefotostock/Contrasto: pages 91, 304, 305
Bonnie B. Pelnar/Corbis: page 485
Jari Peltomaki/NHPA/Photoshot: page 508
Doug Perrine/Auscape: pages 474-475
Doug Perrine/Naturepl.com/Contrasto: pages 27, 372, 380-381, 392, 404-405, 439, 445
Doug Perrine/SeaPics.com: pages 10-11, 353, 362-363, 374-375, 386-387, 393, 408-409, 436, 437, 438-439, 478, 479, 482
Robert L. Pitman/SeaPics.com: page 268
Fritz Poelking/Agefotostock/Contrasto: pages 148, 290-291
Fritz Poelking/Agefotostock/Marka: page 679
F. Poelking/Blickwinkel: page 135
F. Poelking/PandaPhoto: pages 248 right, 249, 646, 676-677, 685
R. Polini/PandaPhoto: pages 306-307
Todd Pusser/Naturepl.com/Contrasto: page 377
Jagdeep Raiput/Ardea.com: pages 510-511

Roger Ressmeyer/Corbis: page 562
Galen Rowell/Corbis: pages 530-531
Galen Rowell/Mountain Light: page 625
Royalty-Free/Corbis: pages 426-427
Jeffrey L. Rotman/Corbis: pages 464-465, 472
Andy Rouse/NHPA/Photoshot: pages 4-5, 206-207, 274-275, 336, 337, 569, 684, 698-699
Carl R. Sams II/Agefotostock/Marka: page 624
Becca Saunders/Auscape: page 361
Francois Savigny/Naturepl.com/ Contrasto: page 137
Phil Savoie/Naturepl.com/Contrasto: page 143
Kevin Schafer: pages 258, 278, 279, 426
Kevin Schafer/Agefotostock/Contrasto: pages 273, 533
Kevin Schafer/Corbis: pages 270-271, 276
Kevin Schafer/zefa/Corbis: pages 272, 714
H. Schmidbauer/Blickwinkel: page 432
Carine Schrurs/Naturepl.com/Contrasto: pages 50-51
SeaPics.com: page 373
Anup Shah/Naturepl.com/Contrasto: pages 31, 100, 100-101, 102-103, 108, 109, 144-145, 153, 160, 164, 164-165, 184, 189, 190, 686-687, 706, 708-709, 710-711, 711
Takemoto Shiratori/NHPA/Photoshot: page 483
Etienne Sipp/Jacana/HachettePhotos/ Contrasto: page 498
Charles Sleicher/DanitaDelimont.com: page 277
Paul A. Souders/Corbis: pages 324, 397, 399
Mark Spencer/Ardea.com: page 452
Jeremy Stafford-Deitsch/SeaPics.com: pages 470-471

Lynn M. Stone/Naturepl.com/Contrasto: pages 496, 497, 726-727
Rosanne Tackaberry/Auscape: pages 320-321
Ron & Valerie Taylor/aArdea.com: page 410
David Tipling/Alamy: page 292
Jim Toomey/Agefotostock/Contrasto: pages 660-661
Steve Toon/NHPA/Photoshot: pages 198, 632
S. Tuengler/Blickwinkel: pages 330-331
Stefano Unterthiner: pages 328, 329, 552
Masa Ushioda/SeaPics.com: pages 400, 401, 404, 473
Ingrid Van Den Berg/Agefotostock/Marka: page 323
Jeff Vanuga/Corbis: pages 242-243
Tom Vezo/Naturepl.com/Contrasto: page 653
Kennan Ward/Corbis: pages 247, 252-253
M. Watson/Ardea.com: page 259
J. Watt/PandaPhoto: pages 376, 383, 388-389, 448
James D. Watt/SeaPics.com: pages 398, 402, 462-463
Dave Watts/NHPA/Photoshot: page 174
Doug Wechsler/Naturepl.com/Contrasto: pages 200 and 200-201
Randy Wells/Corbis: pages 248 left, 539
Start Westmorland/Corbis: page 456
Doc White/SeaPics.com: page 266
Staffan Widstrand/Naturepl.com/ Contrasto: pages 221, 594, 600, 601, 616-617
Winfried Wisniewski/Agefotostock/ Contrasto: page 563
K. Wothe/Blickwinkel: pages 150-151
Robert Yin/SeaPics.com: pages 460-461
Günter Ziesler: pages 534-535
Cover: Eric Baccega Naturepl.com/ Contrasto
Back Cover: Michel and Christine Denis Huot

• Alaska. For the last 10,000 to 20,000 years, the polar bear has been the Far North's mightiest predator.

Cover • Alaska. The seasonal abundance of fish makes finding food easy for this brown bear.

Back cover • Africa. This leopard's yawn could be due to either sleepiness or hunger.